Sunset

BARBECUE
COOK BOOK

By the editorial staffs of
Sunset Books & Sunset Magazine

LANE BOOK COMPANY
Menlo Park, California

About this book

This book is written for barbecuers of every degree of skill.

Nearly every recipe within its covers was created by a charcoal chef, proudly submitted to *Sunset* Magazine, and there passed  through the test of fire. Each recipe was first checked over by a skeptical home economist, and if it didn't sound too outlandish, it was turned over to a veteran barbecuer to cook over charcoal. Then the acid test: the cooked delicacy was tried on a panel of suspicious folk who love barbecued meat in all its guises. Recipes that survived this ordeal were published in *Sunset* and are here assembled in book form.

A glance at this assortment will show that, collectively, the barbecue chef is a nimble, versatile craftsman.

Here are recipes for broiling over, on, and under live coals; for roasting underground, in foil, or on a spit; for baking trout in mud, chicken in foil, tuna in gunny sacks, salmon in chicken wire. Here are 40 savory combinations to thread on skewers; and a score of budget-balancers starring hamburger and the faithful hot dog, to alternate with 14-carat steaks. You'll find recipes to feed 300, for a crowd of 25, for your family, for just yourself. There is a challenging selection of sauces that range from the simple button-of-garlic in oil to lengthy formulas that sweep the spice shelf clean.

A final chapter on foods that make good partners with barbecued meats offers a selection of casseroles, skillet fare, breads, salads, relishes, and savory butters.

This second edition is considerably expanded over its immediate predecessor. Both editions are lineal descendants of what is probably the first book ever published on home barbecuing—the *Sunset Barbecue Book* of 1938.

L. C. No. 57-8904

Fourth Printing June 1960

Contents

The Art of barbecuing

It takes just one or two good whiffs of the aroma of meat sizzling on an open grill and just one or two good mouthfuls of juicy barbecued steak to make a man want to try his own hand at barbecue cookery. And once he dons cap and apron, he is on his way to becoming a master chef.

The beginning barbecuer will be generously loaded down with instructions by his experienced friends; but he has no need to be discouraged by their apparent expertness, for the techniques are easily learned. The novice should have no trouble in mastering this deft art once he has learned how to control his fire, how to make the most out of his equipment, how to cook which kinds of meat, and how to plan a meal.

Firemanship

At least half of barbecuing is not cooking at all. It comes under the general heading of "firemanship"—which means getting the fire to start in the first place, keeping it going neither too fast nor too slow, maneuvering the meat so the fire—or the smoke—gives it just the right treatment, testing its temperature, making adjustments, keeping fuel and all equipment in working order for the next time.

The Right Kind of Fire

The beginner often makes the mistake of trying to cook over open flame instead of waiting for coals to form. Only coals that have been allowed to burn to a gray color, shot with a ruddy glow, give the even, constant heat needed for barbecuing.

The distinctive flavor of barbecued meat comes less from the smoke of the burning fuel (some charcoal briquets give off no scent) than from the singeing of the meat's surface and from the smoke that rises from the smouldering meat drippings.

If a wood-smoke flavor is desired, there are several ways of obtaining it. Liquid smoke may be included in the marinade or basting sauce. With skill, the meat may be grilled before the bed of coals has fully formed and while the fuel is still giving off some smoke; or wood that is slightly damp or green may be used. Favorite method is to toss a few chips of aromatic wood or leaves on the coals just before the meat is removed from the barbecue. Favorite aromatic varieties are oak, hickory, bay, alder, myrtle, and the orchard woods such as apple, lemon, orange, and cherry. Some kinds are too zestful—eucalyptus gives meat a medicinal flavor, pine imparts a turpentine taste.

Charcoal as a Barbecue Fuel

Charcoal is obtainable in either lump or briquet form. Briquets produce uniform heat, yield long-lasting coals, and burn without sparking. However, the lump style is cheaper and gives off a truer wood aroma than briquets.

Charcoal briquets may look alike, but different brands perform in different ways. As rough temperature tests made at *Sunset* show (see chart), some brands start up promptly, reach cooking heat in record time, and then die down quickly; others follow an opposite pattern. Of course, knowledge about these variations is useful

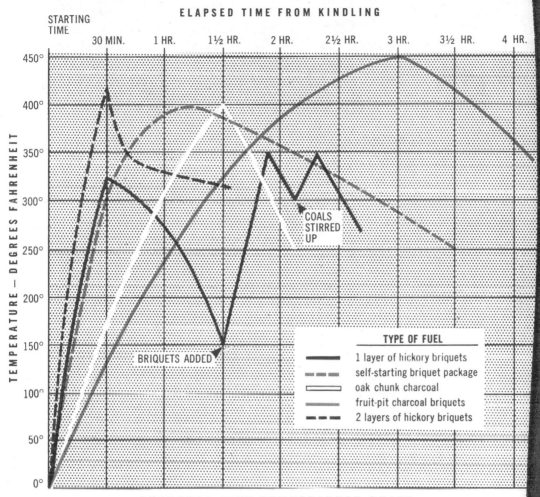

STARTING
TIME

30 MIN. 1 HR. 1½ HR. 2 HR. 2½ HR. 3 HR. 3½ HR. 4 HR.

450°
400°
350°
300°
250°
200°
150°
100°
50°
0°

TEMPERATURE — DEGREES FAHRENHEIT

COALS
STIRRED
UP

BRIQUETS ADDED

TYPE OF FUEL
1 layer of hickory briquets
self-starting briquet package
oak chunk charcoal
fruit-pit charcoal briquets
2 layers of hickory briquets

CHARCOAL TIME-TEMPERATURE CHART

to the barbecuer. Where he has the choice, he can select a quick-heat type for steaks or hamburgers, and a slow-burning kind for spit roasting. It may pay you to experiment with the heat output of the various brands obtainable in your locality. (A grill thermometer with a range of 0° to 500°, or better 700°, will do.)

How much charcoal? Most beginners make the mistake of using far more charcoal than they need. You don't need to cover the entire firebed with briquets unless you expect to use the whole grill. Just make the charcoal layer a little wider all around than the area of the food to be cooked. Small, efficient barbecues, such as the Skotch Grill and hibachi, will perform capably with a handful of charcoal.

Fire Control

The following recommendations apply principally to charcoal briquets, but may be adjusted to chunk charcoal or wood embers.

Preparing the firebed: Briquets burn from the bottom to the top, hence require draft from below. If your barbecue unit is designed with an open-work grate, the draft is taken care of. But if you are broiling on a barbecue with a solid metal firebox—such as a brazier bowl—cover it with a level layer of sand or gravel. This partly protects the metal from the intense heat of the charcoal; and it facilitates cleaning the unit, because the sand rather than the metal collects the grease and ashes. Gravel provides better bottom draft than sand, and it may be washed in hot water and re-used after it has been spread and dried in the sun (be sure it's dry before you use it again—wet gravel will pop).

If you don't like the messiness of a barbecue fire, line the firebox with heavy aluminum foil. It will increase the radiant heat. Afterwards, lift out the whole thing—ashes, meat drippings, and all— and discard it in the garbage can.

Starting the fire: Charcoal is regarded as a stubborn fuel, but there are several proven ways of coaxing it into flame:

1. Kindling will often start it burning. Build a paper and kindling fire tepee fashion and when it is burning drop charcoal on it. Or, arrange charcoal around the kindling pile before lighting paper. Or, build the fire on top of charcoal. All these methods are slow, and you will probably need to encourage the coals with blowing, a fireplace bellows, an air mattress or bicycle pump, or, for heroic measures, the blower on your vacuum cleaner.

2. Electric starters work quickly on most types of charcoal. You merely set the hot coil on top of the briquets and they will begin to glow in a few minutes.

3. Liquid starters are simple and effective to use. Choose any fluid sold specifically for starting a barbecue fire, alcohol, or any relatively odorless paint thinner or cleaning solvent. Neither kerosene nor gasoline is recommendable for this purpose: the strong odor of kerosene is too likely to linger, gasoline has no place around any fire.

Liquid starters may be applied in two ways: (1) You can pour a ½ cup on the briquets, arranged in a pyramid, wait a few minutes, then throw a lighted match onto the dampened charcoal. (2) Or you can pre-soak a few, arrange them at the base of a pyramid, and light them. To pre-soak, immerse them in a coffee can until they stop bubbling. Some barbecuers keep a dozen or so "marinated" briquets in a sealed can or jar, so they can start a fire without delay.

Another method is to soak a brick with starter fluid, stack briquets around it, and light it. Remove it after the fire is going.

4. Pre-ignition can sometimes be used to advantage, particularly with a kitchen barbecue. Place a few briquets in a wire basket or frame and set over an open gas flame until they are ignited, then transfer to the barbecue firebed.

5. A "kindle can" will give you quick results. This is simply a tin chimney in which you can efficiently start charcoal burning. You can buy them ready-made or you can easily make one from an empty 2-pound coffee can. Remove the bottom, and with a beer can opener, punch 4 legs around the bottom by bending the tabs of metal in and all the way down. Between the legs, punch 4 air vents— leaving the metal tabs sticking straight in.

Set the can on your barbecue firebed, put in it 4 or 5 marinated briquets or a crushed milk carton, and fill the can with briquets. Light the carton or the starter briquets, and wait about 15 minutes, or until coals are glowing. Then remove can with tongs or pliers (you can use it over and over again), spread the coals on the firebed, or add fresh coals around the edge of the pilot fire if you need large coverage.

Temperature measurement: A grill thermometer (obtainable in patio shops) is the most accurate way to tell when the fire is at the cooking temperature. Veteran barbecuers recommend 350-375° for steaks, hamburgers, lamb chops, kebabs, and fish; 300-

325° for pork and poultry. A thermometer that you can clamp to the turning spit will let you keep track of the fire for a spit-roasting. Air temperature at that level should be above 300° for proper cooking.

You can also be your own thermometer. Just hold your hand at "meat level" (grill or spit height) and count seconds until the heat makes you remove your hand. Use a watch with a sweep-second hand or one of the many photographers' methods for counting seconds ("one sub-one, two sub-two, etc."). As a general rule, if you can hold your hand over the heat for less than 3 seconds, the fire is ready for barbecuing.

Fire control: If you want low heat, use tongs to space out the coals so they won't touch, in a kind of checkerboard pattern.

To eliminate those annoying flareups from fat drippings, arrange your fire in a ring, on sand. Put your meat on the spit or grill so the drippings will fall on the bare sand inside the circle of fire. The heat of such a fire will be just about as even as that of the usual bed of coals, and it is likely to do a better-than-usual job of cooking the outside edges of meat.

If you need more heat, flick the white ashes off the tops of the coals and you nearly double their heat for the next 5 minutes or so. To add fuel, introduce it from the edge of the fire; don't put fresh briquets on top of those that are already burning.

Dousing flames: You often have to act fast if you don't want your meat charred. A sprinkler bottle is effective in quenching flame, but it tends to kick up ash and it may put on too much water and steam the meat. A water pistol has some of the disadvantages of the sprinkler, but it is more fun to use and more accurate. You can also use a water soaked rag on a stick, if your fire is accessible. A unique method is to lay a lettuce leaf over the flame—the flame subsides and the lettuce disintegrates.

Dousing the coals: Many times, after you are through cooking, there is plenty of fuel value left in the charcoal. It is easily saved. Either toss with tongs into a water-filled bucket or into an old, riddled bucket or paint can and run water through. Let them dry out thoroughly before attempting to barbecue with them.

Shopping for Barbecue Meats

The answer to the old question, "What can we barbecue?" is not as simple as it might seem. Spareribs, steak, chicken, and hamburgers may be the time-tested favorites of many barbecuers, but the list of meats that can be deliciously cooked over a fire of glowing coals is much longer. Actually, you can barbecue literally anything that can be pan fried or broiled or oven roasted indoors.

Since some barbecue "naturals" may be strangers to your in door range, here is a description of old-time favorites and the many tempting alternates.

Steak From the Loin

Of all the major cuts of beef, the loin is by far the most tender and the most expensive. From it are taken the five standard steaks pictured on following pages: sirloin, pinbone, porterhouse, T-bone, and club.

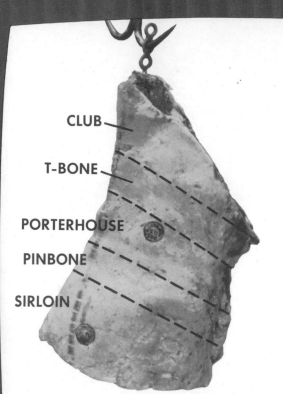

CLUB

T-BONE

PORTERHOUSE

PINBONE

SIRLOIN

Selecting exactly the right steak is part of the fun of planning a barbecue. Your basic choices are shown to the left. To help you identify what your meatman shows you, the loin was cut into steaks, pictured below. The flank, kidney, and some fat were previously removed from the 53½-pound cut. Each steak was cut 1½ inches thick—size most cooks prefer for grilling. Thickness determines the number of steaks you can cut from loin. Total weight of trimmed steaks, 42 pounds; meat trim for ground beef, 3 pounds; waste fat for salvage, 8½ pounds. The total number of steaks, 17

If the loin is boned before it is cut into steaks, there are two other choices: the fillet and the New York cut. The portion of the meat above the bone is called the New York strip; the meat below the bone is the fillet or tenderloin. The rest of the meat on the loin goes into ground beef or stewing meat.

All of these steaks, with two exceptions, are about equally tender. The first of the sirloin steaks (the one that is next to the

SIRLOIN	PINBONE	PORTERHOUSE	T-BONE	CLUB
18 lbs.-4 oz.	6 lbs.-5 oz.	9 lbs.-4 oz.	5 lbs.-3 oz.	3 lbs.

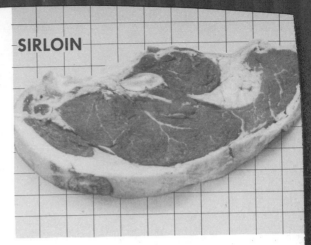

SIRLOIN

Family-size steak, which includes a fair-sized tenderloin, a large section of loin, and a comparatively small amount of bone. These are sometimes named for shape of bone—round bone or flat bone. Since families are smaller today, sirloin is often boned to make boneless New York strip steaks, choice filet mignon

round) is a little "rough" because part of it is cut with the grain of the meat instead of against it. This steak isn't quite so tender as the sirloin next to it. The other exception is the fillet, the most tender steak of all.

Steaks up to about 2½ inches in thickness can be grilled over coals, and any thicker cut from the loin can be roasted on a spit or in a smoke oven.

The grade of beef determines the tenderness and juiciness of your steaks. Steak that is cut from choice grade beef is well marbled (tiny lines of fat running all through the meat), and the outside fat is white. Such beef has been scientifically fed so there will be an even distribution of fat all over the animal. In addition, today's beef is much plumper and stockier than the steers that used to go to market. As a result, there is a much larger percentage of edible meat in relation to bone in all top quality beef.

When you ask for choice beef, you can expect to be shown steaks (or roasts) that have a large amount of fat on the outside and in the meat. If the fat isn't there, the steak isn't choice grade, and it will be dry, less flavorful, and less tender. Actually, much of

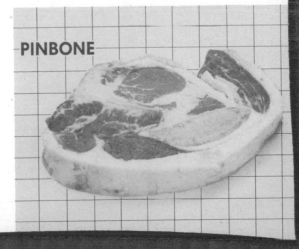

PINBONE

This steak has largest tenderloin, but it also has largest amount of bone, so it costs less per pound. It is sometimes called a hip steak because of the oval-shaped pin (or hip) bone in it. It is sometimes trimmed, boned out and sold as a porterhouse steak. More often it is cut, like sirloin, into boneless steaks

PORTERHOUSE

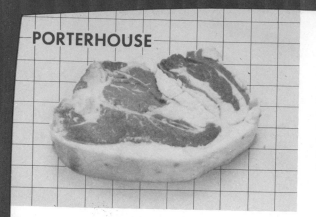

Porterhouse is a choice steak because it contains a good-sized tenderloin. It is sometimes sold as T-bone. The only difference between it and usual T-bone is that tenderloin is larger. You can cut fillet and New York steaks out to cook separately and grind "tail" into choice ground beef—delicious grilled

the fat on choice beef goes to salvage and isn't passed on to you. The waste on this grade of beef will run from 35 to 40 per cent of the total weight. Naturally, part of this waste is figured into the cost of the steak.

Before the steak is weighed, it is also trimmed. Not only is the fat evened up, but part of the "tail" is usually cut off. This piece of less tender meat goes into ground beef or stew meat. The price difference between ground meat and top quality meat is also figured into the total cost of your steak.

Standing Rib

Next to the loin, the rib is the most useful major cut of beef for

Those steaks from the second third of short loin are called the T-bone because of the shape of the bone. As each steak is removed from loin, the tenderloin (the meat below the bone) gets smaller until it almost disappears. If steak is cut 1½ inches thick, broil (3 inches below heat) 9 minutes each side for rare

The balance of short loin is made up of club steaks, which have little or no tenderloin. These are individual steaks unless cut very thick. If the tail is left on, it is called a short-cut steak. These are next to the standing rib cut. It is from the standing rib that bone-in rib steaks and tender market steaks come

T-BONE

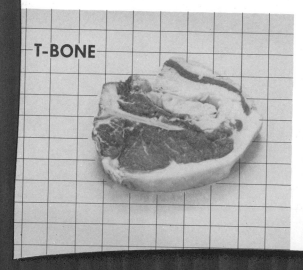

CLUB

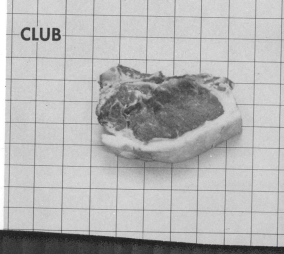

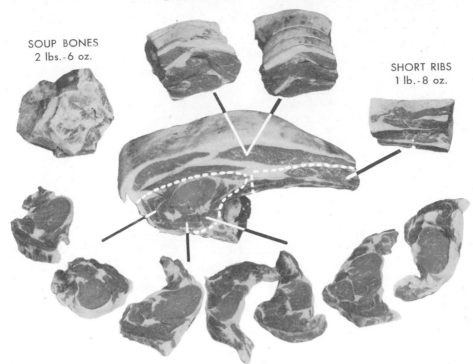

2 POT ROASTS - 4 lbs.-12 oz.

SOUP BONES
2 lbs.-6 oz.

SHORT RIBS
1 lb.-8 oz.

7 MARKET STEAKS - 3 lbs.

RIB ROAST PLAN NUMBER 1. *Seven delicious market steaks, 1 long-rolled pot roast or two small ones, enough short ribs for a barbecue, and a variety of meaty soup bones were cut from 10-inch rib roast. Weight: 13 lbs., 4 oz.*

the barbecuer. The standing rib can be roasted or cut into steaks for broiling, but that isn't the limit to the rib's versatility. The photos here and on the next page show two ways of cutting the rib into a variety of cuts, most of which are suitable for outdoor cooking.

Steak hungry? Take a look at Rib Roast Plan Number 1. You can have choice market steaks, 2 pot roasts, short ribs, and soup bones.

Roast beef a rarity on your table lately? Check Rib Roast Plan Number 2. You can dine on rare spit-roasted beef, put away enough cube steaks and short ribs for several meals, and have meaty bones for soup.

Starting point for both plans is the full length (10-inch) 2-rib roast. Whichever Rib Roast Plan you choose, you'll save money because the full 10-inch cut is always less expensive than the standard, shorter 7-inch cut. Once you try either of these plans, chances are you'll graduate from the 2-rib roast to a 3-rib, because you'll get even more meat at the same lower price per pound. For instance, a 3-rib 10-inch roast will cut into 9 or possibly 10 market steaks plus two large-sized pot roasts and enough short ribs to serve six in a generous fashion.

An extra dividend of these two meat plans is that the tender meat is separated from the less tender. Market steaks and cut-down roasts are equally tender throughout because they come from the "eye" of the meat. The tougher outside parts are "cubed" to tenderize the fibers or rolled together for pot roasting.

The standing rib roast used in either plan must be cut off the heavy end of a whole standing rib. The smaller end has too much bone and too little meat to work with. Should you decide to buy a whole standing rib (7 or 8 ribs) to put in your freezer,

RIB ROAST PLAN NUMBER 2. *A good-sized rib roast which includes only tender "eye" meat, as well as 14 cube steaks, meaty short ribs, and soup bones were cut from 2-rib, full-length standing rib roast which weighed 12 pounds*

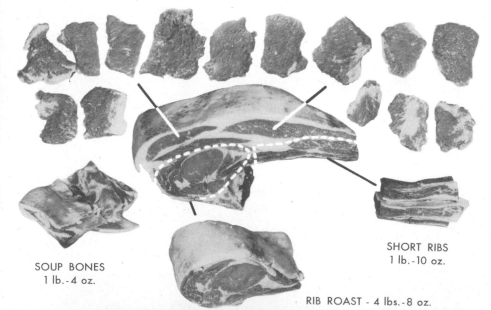

CUBE STEAKS - 3 lbs. - 6 oz.

SOUP BONES
1 lb. - 4 oz.

SHORT RIBS
1 lb. - 10 oz.

RIB ROAST - 4 lbs. - 8 oz.

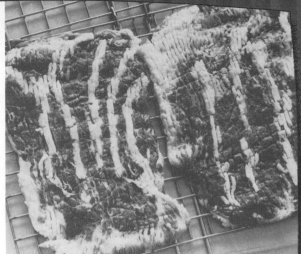

TOP ROUND STEAK. *Relatively tender meat with good grain, flavor. Grill, basting if desired. If steak is thick (2 to 3 inches), slice across grain to serve*

FLANK STEAK. *This thin, lean cut of meat needs special preparation for broiling. Have butcher strip suet across steaks, then run through the tenderizer*

ask to have the heavy end cut according to either of the plans, and then use the smaller end for rib steaks and a 7-inch standing roast with all the bone left in. You'll still have all the short ribs left for barbecuing.

Naturally, you can't expect to walk into your meat market and ask to have a rib roast cut up following either plan with the same

SHORT RIBS. *This is a self-basting cut of meat because it has streaks of fat running through the lean. Short ribs can be skewered or cooked right on the grill*

CHUCK STEAKS. *Tough cut needs tenderizing salt to make it suitable for broiling. Top chuck, center cross rib cuts make best steaks for barbecuing*

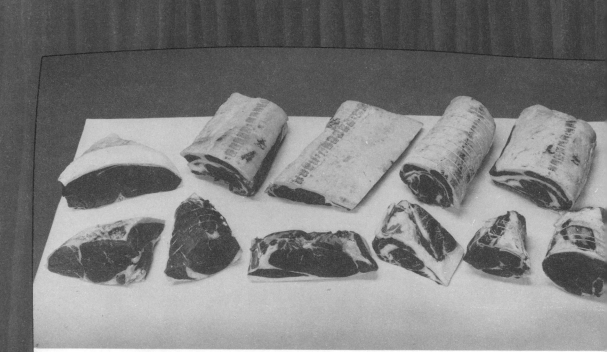

These are 11 of the beef roasts that you can roast on a spit or in a Chinese oven. The lineup, from left to right: (top row) top round, Spencer, New York strip, rolled rib, standing rib; (bottom row) rump, sirloin tip, top sirloin, mar- *ket ("eye" of rib), double tenderloin, and cross rib. Price varies widely— rump, cross rib the lowest, tenderloin and New York strip the highest. Price depends upon quality of beef, amount of fat and bone in cut, and tenderness*

casualness you use when buying a pound of ground chuck. Your meat cutter needs some advance notice because it takes time to cut, saw, slice, tie, and wrap the meat.

When you wrap the various cuts for freezing, don't forget the unexpected guest. Put away a few single servings.

HAMBURGER. *Normally, you can buy 3 grades of ground beef for this traditional favorite. Ground round, chuck, economy-priced ground beef all used. Many chefs find ground round too lean (and expensive) for barbecuing, but the other two are satisfactory broiled*

LAMB

For some barbecuers, the tender meat of spring lamb has no peer when it comes to outdoor cooking. Whether it is lean chunks cut from the leg and skewered with green pepper and onion in the centuries-old tradition of Armenian cookery, or a boned loin roast, or chops, or spareribs, if the meat is good lamb, almost any cut can be cooked over the coals. Only the neck, the square-cut shoulder, and the shank are too tough for barbecuing without special preparation.

The less tender cuts of lamb come from the forequarter, and the picture below shows the variety of cuts than can be taken from this

From a forequarter of lamb weighing 12 to 15 pounds, a family of two can get 7 hearty meals with plenty of extra meaty chops, breast of lamb for guests.

This forequarter has been cut in one of several ways suitable for the barbecue. Rib rack, shoulder pieces could have been left uncut to be roasted on the spit

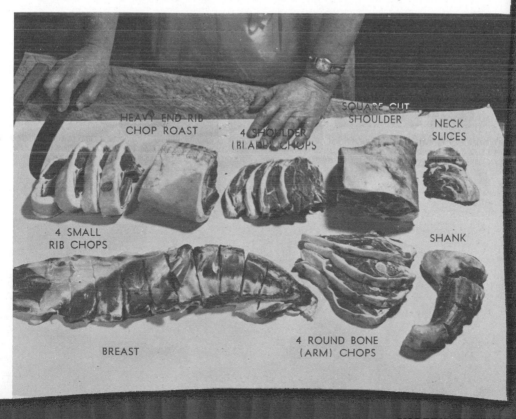

HEAVY END RIB
CHOP ROAST

SQUARE CUT
SHOULDER

NECK
SLICES

4 SHOULDER
(BLADE) CHOPS

4 SMALL
RIB CHOPS

SHANK

BREAST

4 ROUND BONE
(ARM) CHOPS

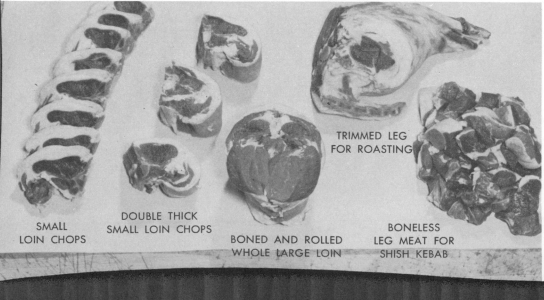

LEGS •
Weight of
both legs
is 11 lbs.

**LARGE
LOIN •**
Total weight
is 5 lbs.

**SMALL
LOIN •**
Total weight
is 6 lbs. 8 oz.

*Hind of lamb provides barbecuers meat
to roast, broil, and skewer. Every part
of cuts shown are excellent barbecued.
Costs more than meat from forequarters*

*Total weight of whole hind of lamb is
22½ pounds. From it were cut small
loin, large loin (boned weight 3 lbs.,
10 ozs.), two legs (approximately 5
lbs., 4 ozs. each). Eight 1-inch-thick
loin chops weigh approximately 6¼*

*ounces each; double-thick, individual
lamb chop roasts weigh almost a pound
apiece. Trimmed leg of lamb weighs
4 pounds, 13 ounces; meat from other
leg, cut in skewering squares, weighs
3¾ pounds after bone, fat are removed*

SMALL
LOIN CHOPS

DOUBLE THICK
SMALL LOIN CHOPS

BONED AND ROLLED
WHOLE LARGE LOIN

TRIMMED LEG
FOR ROASTING

BONELESS
LEG MEAT FOR
SHISH KEBAB

SHISH KEBAB. *Great favorite made from well-marinated squares of lamb from leg threaded onto skewer with onion, tomato, green pepper. Beef, fish occasionally used. Shish means skewer; kebab, broil. Cook 35 to 40 minutes*

BREAST OF LAMB. *Here breast is cut in two for easier handling. This very inexpensive cut should be thoroughly cooked to render out excess fat. Cook spareribs over low coals, turning occasionally until meat is tender and glazed*

section. All but the shoulder cut in the upper right hand corner are ready for the barbecue. Actually, the meat from the shoulder will make acceptable shish kebab if taken from a choice lamb and well marinated before skewering.

The choicest cuts of lamb come from the hindquarter—the leg and both the large and small loin. Since meat from the hindquarter is preferred by most, it costs more per pound than cuts from the forequarter.

If you have a freezer, you might consider buying a whole hind or forequarter of lamb. The meat costs you less per pound than if you buy the separate cuts, and lamb gives you a wide range of barbecue choices.

If you buy yearling lamb, don't count on the meat being as tender and succulent as spring lamb. Mutton is even more strongly flavored but, properly prepared, it can be deliciously barbecued. The best indications of a lamb's age are the fat and bones. The younger a lamb is, the whiter its fat and the pinker and softer its bones.

When you think of lamb for the barbecue, don't forget the liver and the kidneys. Both are easily and temptingly prepared over the coals.

PORK

Pork spareribs rank as one of the all-time favorites with the barbecuing fraternity. The ribs can be grilled, spitted, or hung in a smoke oven, and after frequent basting with a spicy basting sauce, they reach a crisp, glazed brown stage—good enough to turn the head of any gourmet.

Many fresh cuts of pork other than the spareribs deserve consideration when you shop for barbecue meat. Any fresh roast or broiling cut can be cooked on an outdoor grill or in a barbecue oven. Though it takes longer to cook a piece of pork thoroughly than it does to cook a piece of beef or lamb of the same weight, the end product may well be more than worth the extra effort.

Some of the more popular cuts of pork for barbecuing: (back row) fresh ham, loin, spareribs; (front row) shoulder, loin chops, sausage, smoked ham steak. The leg, shoulder, and loin take slow roasting to cook properly. Parboil the sausage before grilling. The ham steak can be grilled right over the coals. If you buy spareribs, remember to have your meatman crack the bones for you

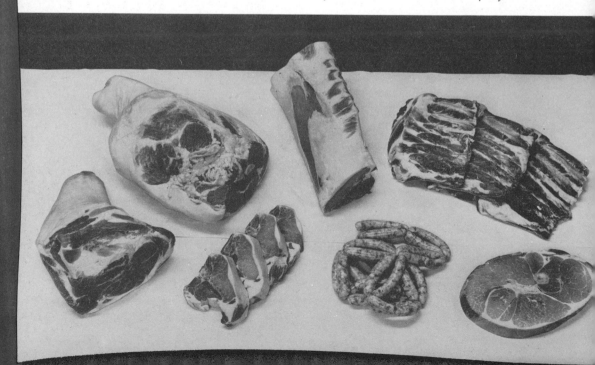

HEAVY FRYERS OR ROASTERS. *Too meaty to split for a single serving. Cut in quarters, marinate, then grill. You can buy chicken parts frozen or fresh, letting your palate and pocketbook act as guides. Always grill with inside down first, then turn to brown skin side. Grill chicken slowly over the coals. Cooking time: 40 minutes to 1 hour*

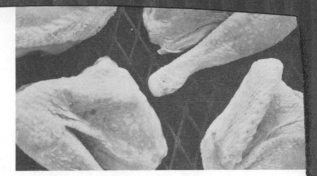

FOWL

Any fowl, except tough stewing birds, can be deliciously broiled or roasted over coals. Remember that fowl tends to be dry and requires frequent basting. To avoid scorching, cook over relatively low coals

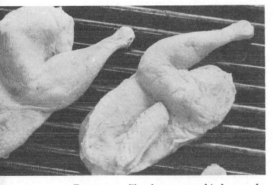

BROILERS. *Tender young birds can be halved or split, boned, and flattened for broiling. Marinate before cooking*

SMALL TURKEYS. *Can be cooked on a rotating spit over moderate coals. Use meat thermometer to check doneness*

CHICKEN LIVERS. *Thread chicken livers on skewers, winding bacon strips over and under. Cooking time: 20 minutes*

SQUAB CHICKENS. *Expensive, delicious. Figure 1 per person. Baste frequently with lemon, butter and wine mixture*

WHOLE FISH. *Some outdoor chefs make a specialty of barbecuing whole fish such as salmon, bass, small tuna.*

This salmon is ready to be wrapped in chicken-wire shield which keeps meat from falling off bones while it cooks

FISH/SEAFOOD

You'll find a wide range of seafoods at your market that can be easily cooked on your barbecue. Any steak or boneless cut may be broiled if you use a toasting rack or hardware cloth tray to prevent the meat from sticking to the grill. Whole fish also need special care to prevent the meat from falling apart.

Fish, like fowl, are usually short on fat and need frequent basting to protect the meat from excessive drying.

FILLETS AND STEAKS. *These cuts can be broiled to a turn if cooked on wire mesh to keep the meat from falling apart*

SHELLFISH. *Lobsters, split and buttered, are delicious grilled. Oysters, prawns, among others, are ideal for skewering*

Broiling
on the grill

The barbecue grill is a versatile cooking device. Any of the meats —steaks, chops, bacon, frankfurters, half chicken, ham slices—that can be broiled or fried on a kitchen range can be cookd on a grill.

Steaks: The proper way to grill steaks is a matter of raging controversy. Many cooks like to broil them quickly, searing them over a hot fire or even slapping them on the coals. Other barbecuers prefer to broil slowly over a coolish fire. Recent research favors the slow school of broiling, but you may wish to try both techniques before choosing sides.

About turning, salting, and basting meat—most barbecuers prefer to turn the meat only once during broiling and to salt at the end of the cooking. Remember not to puncture the meat when you turn it, for this lets the rich juices sizzle into the fire. Flip it over gently with a pair of cooking tongs or a spatula. If you must use a fork, jab it into the fat rather than the lean portion of the meat.

Steaks can be served with only salt, pepper, and butter for seasoning—and many barbecuers feel this way is best—but some like to sharpen the flavor by soaking the meat ahead of time in a marinade or by basting on the grill with a favorite barbecue sauce. You will find sauce recipes that span the full taste spectrum, but you are well advised to start off with the gentler ones and graduate to the hair-raising mixtures.

Fish, fowl: Fish can be deliciously broiled, but they are tricky to handle because they tend to stick to the hot grid, even when it has been well greased. To overcome this, wrap fish in leaves or aluminum foil, or place in a wire grilling frame.

Broilers cut in half will grill well, but they tend to dry out if they are not basted frequently. Grill first with the skin side down. Flavor may be improved by marinating.

Fruits and vegetables: Most fruits and vegetables can be grilled with surprisingly tasty results. They tend to burn, however, unless wrapped in foil, basted frequently, or kept rotated. Corn is best.

In general: Before cooking on the grill, grease it with a piece of suet or a rag dipped in cooking oil. This prevents meat from "freezing" to the hot metal. Many experts recommend that you let the grill stay dirty after using—next time, heat it up, brush the grease loose, and wipe clean with paper towels.

Quenching flare-ups can be fun with an ordinary water pistol. Water may be directed precisely where needed. Other methods: sprinkler bottle, lettuce leaf

Use tongs to turn over steaks when broiling them on the grill. Better than cooking fork, which punctures meat, causes juices to run out. Turn only once

ABOVE. *Uncracked lamb shanks (previously parboiled until just tender) broil on grill inside fireplace. Shanks freely brushed with well-seasoned baste.*
RIGHT. *Bananas follow lamb on grill. Fruit is slit open and filled with a butter and orange concentrate mixture*

For basting meat on grill, try "brush" composed of celery stalk, few green onion tops, sprig each of fresh thyme and rosemary, tied together at base

Variety of Meat	Cut of Meat	Size or Weight	Warm-up Time for Frozen Meat		Recommended Heat of Fire*
			In Refrigerator to 40°	In Room 40° to 70°	
BEEF	Steak	1 Inch	8 Hrs.	4 Hrs.	Hot
	Steak	1½ Inches	9½ Hrs.	5 Hrs.	Hot
	Steak	2 Inches	10½ Hrs.	7 Hrs.	Medium to Hot
	Steak	2½ Inches	12 Hrs.	10 Hrs.	Medium to Hot
	Flank Steak	Whole	8 Hrs.	2½ Hrs.	Hot
	Hamburger	1 Inch	8 Hrs.	3 Hrs.	Medium to Hot
	Tenderloin	Whole	12 Hrs.	10 Hrs.	Medium
FISH	Steak	1 Inch	If frozen, do not thaw.		Medium
	Steak	1½ Inches	"		Medium
	Fillets or Split	Small	"		Medium
	Fillets or Split	Large	8 Hrs.	4 Hrs.	Medium
HAM	Slice	1 Inch	8 Hrs.	4 Hrs.	Low to Medium
	Slice	1½ Inches	9½ Hrs.	5 Hrs.	Low to Medium
LAMB	Chops or Steaks	1 Inch	8 Hrs.	4 Hrs.	Medium
	Chops or Steaks	1½ Inches	9½ Hrs.	5 Hrs.	Medium
	Chops or Steaks	2 Inches	10½ Hrs.	7 Hrs.	Medium
LOBSTER	Split	1 to 2½ Pounds	If frozen, do not thaw.		Medium to Hot
PORK	Chops or Steaks	1 Inch	8 Hrs.	4 Hrs.	Low to Medium
	Chops or Steaks	1½ Inches	9½ Hrs.	5 Hrs.	Low to Medium
	Chops or Steaks	2 Inches	10½ Hrs.	4 Hrs.	Low to Medium
	Spareribs	Whole	7 Hrs.	3 Hrs.	Very Low
POULTRY	Chicken	Split	10 to 12 Hrs.	6 Hrs.	Medium
	Cornish Hen	Split	8 to 11 Hrs.	2 to 3 Hrs.	Medium
	Duck	Split	11 to 12 Hrs.	6½ Hrs.	Medium to Low
	Squab	Split	8 to 11 Hrs.	2 to 3 Hrs.	Medium
	Turkey	Split (3½ to 6 lbs.)	12 to 16 Hrs.	8 Hrs.	Medium
VEAL	Steaks or Chops	1 Inch	8 Hrs.	4 Hrs.	Medium
	Steaks or Chops	1½ Inches	9½ Hrs.	5 Hrs.	Medium
VENISON	Steaks or Chops	1 Inch	8 Hrs.	4 Hrs.	Hot
	Steaks or Chops	1½ Inches	9½ Hrs.	5 Hrs.	Hot
	Steaks or Chops	2 Inches	10½ Hrs.	7 Hrs.	Medium to Hot

* Hot fire, 375° and over; medium, 325°; slow, 200 to 275°. Check with thermometer.

Temperature Chart

Approximate Time for Cooking (each side)						Comments
Very Rare	Rare	Med.-rare	Medium	Well-done		
4 Min.	5 to 6 Min.	7 Min.	7 to 8 Min.	10 Min. or More	1	1. May be cooked frozen if desired medium or well done.
5 Min.	6 to 7 Min.	8 to 9 Min.	10 Min.	12 to 15 Min.	1	To ascertain degree of doneness, cut steak near center with sharp knife.
to 8 Min.	8 to 10 Min.	10 to 15 Min.	15 to 18 Min.	20 Min. or More	1	
to 12 Min.	12 to 15 Min.	15 to 17 Min.	18 to 23 Min.	25 Min. or More	1	
3 to 4 Min.	4 to 5 Min.	5 to 6 Min.	———	———	2	2. Will not be tender unless very rare or rare.
3 Min.	4 Min.	5 Min.	6 Min.	7 Min. or More		
0 to 12 Min.	12 to 15 Min.	15 to 17 Min.	18 to 23 Min.	———	3	3. Should be served rare.
———	———	———	———	3 to 5 Min.	4	4. Do not overcook lest fish become dry. When fish flakes easily with a fork it is done. Internal temperature 135° to 150°.
———	———	———	———	4 to 6 Min.	4	
———	———	———	———	3 to 6 Min.	4	
———	———	———	———	6 to 9 Min.	4	
———	———	———	———	15 to 18 Min.		
———	———	———	———	18 to 23 Min.		
———	4 to 5 Min.	6 Min.	6 to 7 Min.	8 Min. or More	5	5. Lamb may be cooked rare to med.-rare. However, it is a matter of taste.
———	5 to 6 Min.	7 Min.	8 to 9 Min.	10 Min. or More	5	
———	6 to 7 Min.	8 Min.	9 to 10 Min.	12 Min. or More	5	
———	———	———	———	12 to 16 Min. in All	6	6. Cook 4 minutes meat side down, then turn. If frozen, cook longer.
———	———	———	———	13 to 18 Min.	7	
———	———	———	———	15 to 23 Min.	7	7. Pork should be well done but juicy. Cooked to 180° to 185° internal temperature.
———	———	———	———	20 to 30 Min.	7	
———	———	———	———	1 to 1½ Hrs. in All	8	8. Turn every few minutes.
———	———	———	———	15 to 30 Min.	9	9. Do NOT overcook.
———	———	———	———	15 to 20 Min.		10. For wild duck have very hot fire and cook rare.
——	4 to 6 Min	6 to 8 Min.	9 to 10 Min.	15 to 25 Min.	10	
——	——	———	———	12 to 18 Min.		
———	———	———	———	20 to 30 Min.		
———	———	———	———	9 to 10 Min.	11	11. Veal should be well done but never dry.
———	———	———	———	12 to 15 Min.	11	12. Some hunters prefer venison rare rather than well done.
4 Min.	5 to 6 Min.	6 to 7 Min.	7 to 8 Min.	10 Min. or More	12	
5 Min.	6 to 7 Min.	8 to 9 Min.	10 Min.	12 to 15 Min. or More	12	
7 to 8 Min.	8 to 10 Min.	10 to 15 Min.	15 to 18 Min.	20 Min. or More	12	

BEEF

Steak With Garlic Oil

Steak (12 oz. to 1 lb. per
    person)
2 cloves garlic

1 cup olive oil
Salt and pepper to taste

Have meat cut from ¾ to 1 inch thick and gashed around the edge about every 4 inches so it won't curl during grilling. Put the garlic to soak in oil the night before the barbecue. Pour the oil into a shallow pan, remove the garlic and dip the steak in the oil, coating both sides. Then place the steak on the grill. When it is about done, season it with salt and pepper.

Top o' the Morning Steak

Steak, medium thick
Olive oil
Salt
Onion salt

Garlic salt
Pepper, freshly ground
Bay leaves

Paint the steak on both sides with olive oil. Sprinkle liberally with seasonings, place on the grill, and cook as desired. Just before removing the meat, quickly burn a spray of bay leaves under one side and then the other.

Teriyaki Steak

1 large clove garlic
  Half of a fresh ginger root
    chopped fine or 1 to 2
    teaspoons minced dry
    ginger root
1 tablespoon sugar

1 tablespoon cider vinegar
½ cup soy
4 tablespoons dry white table
    wine
2 pounds top round steak

Mash garlic and ginger in a bowl. Dissolve sugar in vinegar; combine with garlic and ginger, and add soy and wine. Marinate steaks in this liquid for several hours, turning occasionally. Grill steaks as desired. Serves 4 to 6.

To impart smoke flavor to grilled steak, add smoke chips to charcoal. Chips are discs of aromatic-burning wood, usually hickory. Chips are often soaked first

Flank steaks, held in hand rack, being broiled in fireplace brazier. Flank steak is a lean, thin cut of meat that needs special preparation for barbecuing. Have meatman lay suet strips across them and run through the tenderizer

Vertical grill permits smokeless broiling because hot fat does not drip into coals. Pan beneath grill catches the drippings, which may be used for gravy. Fine for fatty meats that tend to smoke

Brandy-Broiled Steaks

About 15 minutes before you get ready to barbecue steaks, sprinkle both sides of the steaks generously with California brandy. Then let them stand in a crock or an enamel plate. Broil over coals. When nearly done, salt both sides to taste.

Steak Marchand de Vins

2 tablespoons chopped shallots	A few drops of lemon juice
1 cup dry red wine	Salt and pepper
1/4 pound butter	Beef marrow
1 teaspoon chopped parsley	4 porterhouse steaks,
3 tablespoons very thick soup stock	1 1/2 inches thick

Put the chopped shallots and the wine in a wide saucepan and cook until the total volume has been reduced by more than half; let cool. Then cream this wine and shallot mixture into the butter, along with the parsley, soup stock, lemon juice, salt, and pepper. The marrow should be poked from 2-inch sections of beef leg bone and poached in salted water for 1 minute before slicing.

Grill the steaks over a wood fire (use dried grape shoots if possible). At the moment of serving, strew small pieces of beef marrow over the steak and pour the sauce over all. Enough sauce for 4 good-sized steaks.

This is a true Bordelaise sauce. It's also excellent on broiled lamb or mutton chops, grilled mushrooms, or liver.

Salt-Broiled Steak

This steak must be boneless, lean meat, from 2 to 3 inches thick. Use a large double grill, or toaster, with long handles that loop together. Place the steak on the grill and cover the top with about half an inch of thoroughly dampened coarse salt (not rock salt). Then put a paper napkin over it. Turn the grill over and cover the other side of the steak in exactly the same way. Close the toaster and put it over a very hot charcoal or wood fire, allowing from 15 to 20 minutes for each side.

Melt 1 or 2 pounds of butter in a large roasting pan and have ready sliced bread (preferably French).

When the steak is done, remove the salt, now a hardened cake. Lift the steak into the hot butter and slice. The meat juices will run into the butter—the salt flavor will not go into the meat. With a fork, dip a slice of the bread into the melted butter and meat juices. Place a slice of beef on each piece of bread. Serve immediately.

Grilled Steak Sandwich

Chives	Small fillet steaks,
Butter	1/4 inch thick
	Hamburger buns

Chop chives fine and mix in melted butter. Place steaks on grill and brush frequently with butter-chives mixture. A few minutes before the steaks are done, toast bun halves on the grill. Butter buns and serve steaks between the halves.

Snoqualmie Steak

1/4 cup butter (1/2 cube)	1/4 teaspoon Worcestershire
1 clove garlic, chopped fine	Top sirloin steak,
1 teaspoon seasoned salt	1 1/2 inches thick
Paprika	6 or 8 frankfurter rolls

Melt butter. Mash garlic and salt together; add to butter with paprika and Worcestershire. As mixture boils, swab the upper side of the steak with it. Turn the steak about four times during the cooking; and swab each time with the butter mixture.

While the steak is cooking, slice 6 or 8 frankfurter rolls in half. Serve up the steak with potatoes that have been cubed raw, unpeeled, and fried with onions in salad oil. Then, paint the rolls with the remaining sauce and toast them over the coals. Enough sauce for 4 servings. Figure on 1/3 pound steak per person.

Boolkoki

This Korean dish, pronounced "Bullgogi," is usually served with plain boiled rice, a cabbage salad, and fruit dessert.

3 pounds lean beef (chuck, sirloin tips, or steak)	4 tablespoons finely chopped green onion
1 cup salad oil	2 cloves garlic, minced
1/4 cup sugar	1/2 teaspoon salt
2 tablespoons soy sauce	1/2 teaspoon pepper
	4 tablespoons sesame seed

Cut beef in rather thin slices or strips. Mix remaining ingredients and pour over meat. Be sure that meat is well covered with sauce. Let stand overnight in refrigerator.

Remove from refrigerator and bring to room temperature. When ready to broil over hot coals, drain off surplus sauce. Cook on narrow-mesh grill or thread on skewers. Baste with sauce as necessary during broiling. Serves 6.

Sliced Sirloin

Instead of individual steaks, try serving your guests ½-inch slices of sirloin, cut from a 2½-inch steak broiled over the coals. Serve with melted butter.

Steak Wohlford

Juice of 3 or 4 lemons	Small pinch of oregano
½ cup salt	½ cup olive oil or salad oil
⅛ cup pepper (or more)	3 or 4 large sirloin steaks,
6 to 8 cloves garlic	1½ inches thick
Good sized pinch of thyme	Bay leaves

Mash garlic in a pestle with salt, or put in a liquidizer with some of the oil. Blend lemon juice, salt, pepper, garlic, thyme, oregano, and olive oil. The finished mixture should be about the consistency of library paste, thicker than the usual marinade. Spread on steaks at least 4 to 8 hours ahead of cooking time.

Use all the marinade mixture, pile one steak on top of the other, and let them stand—the longer the better. Do not forget to coat both sides of the bottom steak.

Make a strong tea of bay leaves, letting the leaves steep in hot water half an hour.

Start a fire of lemon wood and let it burn until practically no flame remains. Just before putting steak on the grill, scrape off practically all vestiges of marinade. Grease the grill well with chunks of beef suet. Coat the steaks lightly with melted beef suet, if you have it, otherwise bacon grease.

Sear steak on both sides and then allow to cook slowly on one side without turning until cooked halfway through, then turn and complete cooking to guests' preference. Continue to baste with melted suet to keep from drying.

Whenever the fat dripping from the meat causes the fire to flame, sprinkle the flame lightly with the bay leaf mixture, using a spray of white sage as a brush. Also, at intervals, place several sprays of white sage on the coals.

NOTE: While almost all the marinade should be scraped off, a little left on makes a thin delicious crust.

Steak Hawaiian

1 clove garlic	Steak
1/2 to 1 cup soy sauce	

Chop the clove of garlic very fine and put it in a large shallow glass baking dish or platter. Add the soy sauce and mix. Marinate your steak in this sauce for about 15 minutes, turning it frequently to thoroughly impregnate the meat with the seasoning. Then barbecue to taste. Do not marinate in a metal utensil as it may affect the flavor. Marinade may be used for other meats.

Marinated Beef Short Ribs

Two days before the barbecue purchase 6 pounds of beef short ribs cut about 3 inches long. Marinate the meat for 48 hours in the following mixture:

1 No. 2 can (2 1/2 cups) tomato juice	1/4 teaspoon each ginger and allspice
1 tablespoon sugar	1 teaspoon celery salt
1 teaspoon Worcestershire	1/2 cup vinegar

Place in the refrigerator and turn the meat frequently. For the last 4 hours, remove from the refrigerator and add 1 finely chopped onion and 1 cut clove of garlic.

Remove the meat from the marinade, and pot-roast it in a Dutch oven on top of the stove or in a covered roasting pan in the oven. Use a minimum of water, and keep the heat low. When almost tender, take out and complete cooking on the grill. Baste with basting sauce described below until brown and slightly crisp. Serve with sauce.

Basting sauce:

While meat is cooking, strain marinade; discard onion and garlic. Mix 1/2 cup of marinade with 1/4 cup of olive oil or drippings. Baste the meat with this mixture while barbecuing.

Sauce for serving:

Use the rest of the marinade to make the following sauce to serve with the meat. Sauté a finely chopped onion until brown; add the marinade and 1 teaspoon each of powdered oregano and cumin. (If these are not available, substitute 2 teaspoons of chili powder.) Boil the sauce down until it is about half the original volume. Serves 8.

Poor Man's Filet Mignon

2 pounds flank or top round steak	2 cloves garlic, finely chopped
1 tablespoon meat tenderizer	1/2 teaspoon freshly ground pepper
1 cup red table wine	

Using a large hunting knife or similar blade, score both sides of the steak with a light chopping motion. Sprinkle the tenderizer evenly on both sides and let steak stand at room temperature for the time specified in the tenderizer package directions. Then pour over the wine, add chopped garlic, and sprinkle on the pepper (no salt). Place in refrigerator until ready to cook.

Grill, brushing with marinade as steak cooks, or pan fry to desired rareness over a quick fire. Serve with French fried onion rings, hot garlic bread, a green salad, and chilled red wine. Serves 4.

Savory Chuck Roast

5 pounds chuck roast, about 2 inches thick	Tenderizer

Sauce:

1 onion	2 tablespoons lemon juice
4 tablespoons olive oil	2 teaspoons hickory smoked salt
1 clove garlic	Tabasco to taste
1/2 cup finely sliced celery	1/2 teaspoon freshly ground black pepper
3/4 cup chili sauce	
3/4 cup catsup	3 tablespoons brown sugar, firmly packed
1/2 cup water	
2 tablespoons Worcestershire	1/2 cup sherry or white or dry red wine
2 tablespoons wine vinegar	
1 teaspoon horseradish	
1 teaspoon prepared mustard	

Treat meat with tenderizer according to manufacturer's directions. Slice onion finely and break into rings. Put olive oil in skillet; add chopped garlic and the onion; sauté until onions are golden brown. Thoroughly mix all remaining ingredients except wine and add to onions when they are brown. Bring to a very slow simmer and continue simmering for 20 minutes. Add wine, increasing amount if necessary so the mixture will have a moderately thick consistency and will be just right for applying with a brush. Simmer for an additional 10 minutes.

With the sauce, thoroughly baste the tenderized chuck roast. Place roast on grill close to a hot barbecue fire and brown on

1 CHUCK ROAST *prepared for barbecue by trimming away bones, most fat, gristle*

Two roasts shown at left produced these individual pieces of lean, boneless beef **2**

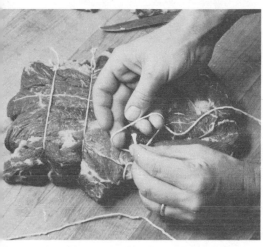

3 *To reassemble lean beef, cross-tie it with strong cord at 1-inch intervals*

Roast in marinating pan. With no bone or gristle, meat is fastened with cord **4**

both sides. Then raise the grill so the roast will get only moderate heat; cover it with the top of a roasting pan, and, turning once, cook until done (2 hours or more depending on heat of fire and degree of rareness you wish). Baste *very* frequently. Cut in thin slices across the grain. Serves 4 to 6.

The sauce may be used either hot or cold. It keeps well in the refrigerator and may also be frozen in freezer cartons for use several weeks later.

Charcoal Roast

4-pound rolled beef roast

Marinade:

5 tablespoons Worcestershire	1 clove garlic, crushed
2 tablespoons Kitchen Bouquet	4 tablespoons soy
	1 cup olive oil

The rolled roast must be cut so it is flat on each end.

Mix together the Worcestershire, Kitchen Bouquet, garlic, and soy in a bowl to make the marinade. Stir well; put roast into the bowl; then rub marinade into the roast with your hands. Cover bowl, place in refrigerator, and let stand for at least 4 hours—overnight is even better.

When you are ready to barbecue, remove cover from bowl containing meat and marinade and pour olive oil over the roast. Again using your hands, rub meat well with the marinade and the olive oil.

Place the roast on the grill so that it is standing on one end. Cook for about 1 hour, basting frequently with the remaining marinade and oil mixture. After a short while, it will turn black; but fear not. At the end of the hour, stand it on the other end and let it continue to cook for a second hour. Serves 8 to 10.

Chuck Roast Teriyaki

7 to 8 pounds chuck roast, about 2 inches thick	Tenderizer

Teriyaki sauce:

1 cup soy sauce	2 cloves garlic
1/4 cup sherry	2 teaspoons sugar (optional)
2 tablespoons ginger root or 1 tablespoon powdered ginger	

Cut all bone and fat from meat and then tie up the lean pieces. (Don't throw away the cuttings; they will help make a good rich soup stock.)

Sprinkle meat liberally with tenderizer and let it stand—follow the manufacturer's directions. Then marinate for about 1 hour in teriyaki sauce.

Finally, broil the meat slowly over a charcoal fire for about 1½ hours, turning only once during the cooking. Serves 8.

Easy Beef Short Ribs

Here's a simple recipe for beef short ribs.

3 pounds short ribs of beef	1/4 teaspoon black pepper
2 tablespoons prepared mustard	1 cup canned tomato juice
1/4 cup vinegar	1 teaspoon salt
	1/2 tablespoon sugar

The day before meat is to be served, pack into a bowl. Beat the other ingredients together and pour over the meat. Cover and let stand overnight. Drain meat and place on grill. Cook slowly, turning meat about every 15 minutes. Serves 4.

Rib Steaks

When barbecuing rib steaks, pound finely minced or crushed garlic into the steaks. Cover with wine vinegar; let stand for several hours at room temperature. Drain and grill.

Chef's Chuck Roast

2 cloves garlic, finely minced	2 tablespoons wine vinegar
2 tablespoons olive oil	4 tablespoons sauterne
1/4 teaspoon dry mustard	Chuck roast, 2 1/2 to 3 inches thick
1 teaspoon soy sauce	
1/2 teaspoon rosemary, crushed, or 1 sprig of the fresh herb	2 tablespoons catsup
	1/2 teaspoon Worcestershire
	1 1/2 teaspoons A-1 sauce

Sauté garlic gently in olive oil, add mustard, soy, and rosemary. Remove from fire and stir in vinegar and wine. Place roast in a bowl and pour sauce over it. During the next 24 hours, turn the meat frequently in the sauce.

Prior to barbecuing, remove the meat and to the remaining sauce add the catsup, Worcestershire, and A-1 sauce. Stir well and apply some of mixture to meat before barbecuing; continue using as a basting sauce during cooking. If the sauce appears too thick, add more olive oil.

The meat should be turned frequently and basted often. A piece of meat 2 1/2 inches thick should be cooked over hot coals for 40 minutes. When served it will be charred outside, rare in the middle. Serves 4 to 6.

Charcoal Broiled Liver 'n Bacon

2 pounds calves liver (approximately 4 pieces cut 1 inch thick)

1 teaspoon monosodium glutamate

8 strips lean bacon

Marinade:

½ cup olive or salad oil
⅛ teaspoon pepper

⅛ teaspoon garlic salt or
¼ teaspoon onion salt

Have the meatman cut liver into 1-inch-thick slices and trim off veins and outer skin. Soak liver in a mild salt-water solution (1 teaspoon salt to 2 cups water) for 30 minutes. Remove and dry surfaces of liver. Sprinkle each side with monosodium glutamate. Take each piece, put a strip of bacon under it and another on top of it, and roll up together and secure with a skewer.

Mix marinade ingredients in a shallow dish or pan. Place liver in marinade, slosh it thoroughly over the meat, and place all in the refrigerator for 2 or 3 hours, turning twice during that time.

Place liver on grill over medium charcoal fire. Broil on each side, turning only once (approximately 15 minutes total cooking time). *Do not overcook.* The meat should be slightly pink on the inside with a mild brown crust on the outside. The bacon drippings that fall on the coals and make the fire flare up give the liver a wonderful barbecue smoke flavor. Serves 4 to 6.

HAMBURGER

Hamburger Cake

Shape seasoned meat into large round cake. Grill over coals, brushing surface with your favorite barbecue sauce during the grilling. Cut into pie-shaped wedges and serve between scones or buns.

Smoky Hamburgers

Broil hamburger patties on each side. Place on lightly toasted buns spread with smoke butter, made by blending ¼ cup of soft butter or margarine with ⅛ teaspoon liquid smoke. Top with thin slices of tomato and onion, and a few mushrooms that have been sliced and sautéed in butter.

Variation:

1 pound ground beef	Salt and freshly ground
½ teaspoon liquid smoke	pepper
1 egg	

Add the liquid smoke and the egg, beaten, to the meat; season, and mix thoroughly. Form into cakes and broil.

Bean-Burger

Place grilled hamburger on toasted bun or French bread slice which has been spread with garlic butter. Top with a generous spoonful of chili beans.

Sweet-Sour Hamburger

For a change try this: Place slice of raw sweet onion on top of grilled hamburger and cover with sugar.

Potato Hamburger

1½ pounds ground beef	1 small onion, chopped
3 medium sized unpeeled raw potatoes, diced	2 tablespoons chopped parsley
	Salt and pepper

Mix together the meat and the unpeeled potatoes; run through the food grinder. Add the chopped onion and parsley; salt and pepper to taste. Shape into medium sized patties and broil. Serve without sauce. Serves 8.

For variety, fry in skillet. Brown flour in the pan juices after frying the patties, add milk, and season with salt and pepper, making a thick milk gravy. Pour the gravy over the patties and serve. A delicious quick gravy can be made by emptying a can of condensed mushroom soup in the cooking pan and thinning slightly with milk.

Grilled Ground Flank

1 pound lean steer flank	1/2 teaspoon each sugar and
1/4 pound steer kidney suet	black pepper
1/4 teaspoon garlic salt	2 tablespoons onion juice
1 teaspoon salt	1/4 teaspoon Tabasco

Grind meat through medium grinder, running it through only once. Mix in other ingredients thoroughly, but lightly, and form into a rectangle about 3 by 6 inches. Place between two pieces of waxed paper and roll lightly with a rolling pin to about ½-inch thickness. Cut into 6 portions, about 2 by 3 inches, and grill. Serves 6.

Hamburger With Milk

2 pounds ground beef	Pinch each of marjoram and
1 egg	mace
3/4 cup milk	Salt and freshly ground
Chopped onion	pepper

Sauce:

3 parts olive oil	Pinch each of sugar, dried
1 part red wine or wine vinegar	marjoram, and rosemary
Trace of thyme and garlic	

Break the egg on the meat, add the milk, onion, and seasonings, and mix and knead well before forming into balls or one large hamburger.

Mix together ingredients for sauce. Baste with sauce during broiling. Serves 8.

Hamburger on the Lean Side

1 pound of beef	1 egg
Salt and freshly ground	1 small can chopped
pepper	mushrooms
A dash of meat sauce	Chopped onions
1/2 teaspoon curry powder	Olive oil
1/2 jigger cognac	

Trim most of fat from the meat before putting it through the grinder. Season with salt, pepper, meat sauce, curry powder, and cognac. Add the egg, mushrooms, and the chopped onions that have been fried to a delicate golden brown in olive oil. Form meat into generous cakes and broil. Serves 4.

Hamburgers make good fireplace fare, but hearth bricks should be covered to protect from grease stains. Home-designed grill above has handle, four legs to keep meat above coals and ashes

Hamburgers should be turned only once, seasoned just before serving. Ground meats less likely to disintegrate and fall into coals if broiled on grill with small mesh or closely spaced rods

Ground Round and Marrow

Have a pound of top round steak passed through the grinder three times with a quarter pound of marrow. Shape meat into cylindrical form. When ready to cook, just cut a thick, liberal slice and place it upon the grill. The marrow will give it a natural flavor and will practically eliminate the necessity for condiments and sauces. Serves 4.

Burgers for Thirty

Form 10 pounds of ground beef into patties. Salt and pepper the hamburgers as they are placed on the grill and brush with the following sauce as they broil:

4 tablespoons olive oil	2 tablespoons Worcestershire
Chopped onion to taste	1 cup wine vinegar
1 cup chili sauce	6 tablespoons brown sugar
1 cup catsup	1 cup water
2 tablespoons dry mustard	Savor salt

Put oil in a skillet, add chopped onion to taste, and brown. Add chili sauce, catsup, mustard, Worcestershire, vinegar, brown sugar, and water. Sprinkle with savor salt and let simmer for 15 minutes. Serves 30.

Hamburger Hot Dogs

Form ground meat into shape of frankfurters. Barbecue as usual. Serve in frankfurter rolls with relishes.

Stretched Hamburger

1 pound ground beef	1 egg
2 carrots, grated	Dash salt and pepper
2 stalks celery, finely chopped	2 tablespoons cooking oil or
1 sprig parsley, finely chopped	shortening
1 green pepper, finely	8 hamburger buns
chopped	1/2 cup melted butter or
1 onion, finely chopped	margarine
1 clove garlic, finely chopped	8 large tomato slices
1 tablespoon steak sauce	Sliced unpeeled cucumber

Mix all ingredients (except the last four listed) together well, using egg as binder. Roll into patties the size of hamburger buns and broil. Split hamburger buns into halves and toast cut sides, then brush with melted butter. Cover each hamburger with one slice of tomato and several slices of fresh, crisp, unpeeled cucumber. A little prepared mustard may be added, if desired. Serves 8.

Beef and Grass

1 pound ground beef	1 tablespoon chopped onion
1 egg	1/2 teaspoon paprika
1 handful each of finely	Salt and freshly ground
chopped spinach and	pepper
watercress	

Break the egg over the meat, add the spinach and watercress, chopped onion, and seasonings, and work together until well blended. Then broil on the grill. (Chopped oysters can also be added to the formula, parsley substituted for watercress.) Serves 6.

Glorified Hamburgers

1 pound ground beef	1 egg
1 cup cracker crumbs	1 small onion, finely chopped
1 cup tomato juice	Salt and pepper to taste

Mix ingredients together. Shape into patties and broil. Serves 6.

Frenchman's Loaf

Split large heated French roll lengthwise. Spread with garlic butter. Place overlapping small, thin, broiled hamburger patties on bottom half of roll; cover with cheese, onion, tomato, and pickle slices. Sprinkle with salt and chili sauce. Add a little finely chopped crisp lettuce and cover with top of roll. Press down firmly. French bread may be used in the same way, cutting the loaf in 4 or 5 pieces.

Hamburger De Luxe

Press ground beef into very thin, flat cakes between waxed paper. Put two cakes together with a filling made from finely chopped raw onion mixed with steak sauce; crimp the edges of the cakes firmly together. Broil over the coals and serve in hot hamburger buns, split and buttered. Cheese slices may be substituted for the onion filling.

Hamburger Doughnuts

Pat out seasoned meat and cut rounds with a doughnut cutter. Grill over coals in usual manner. Serve on buns, filling the center hole with relish or melted cheese.

Spicy Cheeseburgers

1 tablespoon each A-1 sauce, Worcestershire, and wine vinegar	1 small onion, grated
Dash of Tabasco	1 clove garlic, mashed or minced
1½ teaspoons salt	2 pounds ground beef
½ teaspoon each pepper, sage, and celery salt	1 cup fine dry bread crumbs
½ cup salad oil	10 slices American cheese, cut ⅛ inch thick and 3 inches square
½ cup catsup	

The day before you expect to use it, mix sauce. Combine the A-1 sauce, Worcestershire, wine vinegar, Tabasco, salt, pepper, sage, celery salt, salad oil, catsup, onion, and garlic in blender or beat well. Mix meat with sauce and bread crumbs. Divide meat into 20 parts; form each piece into a thin patty. Put 2 patties together with a slice of cheese between them; pinch edges together to seal. Grill on barbecue until meat is browned on both sides. Serves 10.

Hamburger in Toast

1½ pounds ground beef	¼ teaspoon salt
½ cup finely chopped yellow cheese	¼ teaspoon mixed celery and garlic salt
1 tablespoon minced onion	Dash of Tabasco

Mix well and shape into square cakes the size of a slice of sandwich bread. Brush with bacon drippings and broil.

Toast white sandwich bread, butter while hot, and stack on cookie sheet at back of grill. Lay finished hamburger upon a slice of prepared toast and pour about a teaspoon of hot barbecue sauce over it. Top with toast and serve immediately. Serves 6.

Chef's Ground Beef

1½ pounds ground lean beef	½ teaspoon monosodium glutamate
1 teaspoon salt	
¼ teaspoon pepper	2 tablespoons butter or margarine

Sauce:

1 tablespoon butter or margarine	1 tablespoon lemon juice
1 tablespoon chopped parsley	⅛ teaspoon salt
	Pepper and paprika

Blend the ground beef, salt, pepper and monosodium glutamate and form into a loaf about 3 inches wide and 1½ inches thick. Spread the butter over the loaf.

For the sauce, melt butter, and add parsley and lemon juice. Mix thoroughly, and add salt and a sprinkling of paprika and pepper.

Broil meat over coals, lowering grill so that the meat is close to the coals. (Extinguish serious conflagrations immediately.) Count on 5 or 6 minutes for each side, carefully turning the meat only once with a broad spatula. The result should be a loaf crusty brown on the outside, deliciously rare inside.

Place the loaf on a sizzling hot platter the instant it comes from the fire, and pour over it the lemon-butter sauce. Slice into individual servings and serve on warm plates without further delay. Serves 3 or 4.

Korean Beef Barbecue

This hot appetizer is easy to prepare when you entertain, for it takes only two minutes to barbecue it over charcoal. Use a very narrow grill or cake rack over the coals so the meat strips will not fall through.

1 pound chuck roast, cut $1\frac{1}{2}$
    to 2 inches thick

Marinade:

2 tablespoons salad oil
4 tablespoons soy
1 teaspoon garlic powder
$\frac{1}{8}$ teaspoon monosodium
    glutamate
$1\frac{1}{2}$ teaspoons vinegar

Pepper
$1\frac{1}{2}$ teaspoons crushed toasted
    sesame seeds
$\frac{1}{4}$ teaspoon cayenne (or less if
    desired)
1 green onion and top, sliced

Cut meat across the grain in very thin slices. If slices are longer than 3 inches, cut them in half. Place meat in a bowl with the marinade. Mix with your hands until well blended. Cover and chill in refrigerator for at least 4 hours.

To cook, place meat strips on a rack over charcoal and barbecue for 1 minute on each side. Meat should be brown but not crusty.

LAMB

Ground Lamb With Pineapple Ring

Onion juice, lighter and gentler than chopped or grated onion, is used to flavor this lamb dish. The method of extracting onion juice is worth noting for use in other recipes.

1 large onion, minced
$1\frac{1}{2}$ teaspoons salt
1 pound ground lamb

2 stalks celery and leaves,
    chopped very fine
4 rings of pineapple
    Paprika

Place onion in a small bowl, sprinkle with salt, and let stand for about $\frac{1}{2}$ hour. Turn onion onto a square of cloth, roll it up, and twist ends to squeeze out onion juice over ground lamb. Add celery and leaves to meat; work with hand to mix well. Divide into 8 portions, then form each into a roll about 3 inches in length. Place meat on the grill and broil until nicely browned. Place pineapple rings on grill and sprinkle them generously with paprika; put on grill during last 10 minutes of cooking. Serves 4.

Lamb Breast, Shanks

Either lamb breast or lamb shanks may be barbecued with rewarding success. Lamb breast may be placed directly on the grill, but lamb shanks should be precooked until tender before grilling. Braise shanks in small amount of water in a stout, covered pan.

Marinate 4 pounds lamb breast or 4 to 6 pounds precooked shanks in:

1 cup orange juice	2 tablespoons sugar
½ cup lemon juice	

For last 2 hours, add ½ cup of chopped, crushed mint leaves to marinade.

Oil the meat well, place on grill over slow fire, and cook until thoroughly browned. While cooking, baste with a sauce made of ½ cup of the marinade mixed with ¼ cup of salad oil. Heat remainder of the marinade and serve as a sauce with the meat.

Gypsy Lamb

Before barbecuing a roast of lamb or chops, rub with salt in which garlic has been mashed. Then place a layer of onion in the bottom of a pan or crock. Put in the meat and pile sliced lemon and sliced onion on top and around sides. Cover and let stand in cool place overnight, or longer if possible. Before cooking, shake plenty of paprika over the meat. The lamb is then ready to be roasted or grilled.

Lamb Choplets

For lamb choplets (stuffed lamb chops), have meatman remove breastbone from breast of lamb. Cut away first 2 or 3 ribs from point end of breast and remove boneless flank end. Cut meat and some fat from trimmings and, with an extra pound of shoulder meat, grind in food chopper. Season with salt, pepper, and ½ teaspoon mace. Then make a pocket in breast and stuff tightly with ground meat. Chill, cut between ribs, and grill over hot coals.

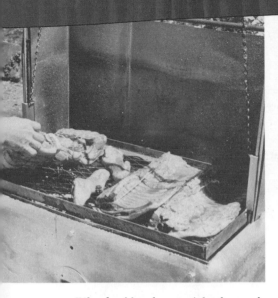 

Rib, shoulder, breast of lamb may be barbecued on the grill. First marinate in sauce, then grill large pieces for 1 hour, turning and basting regularly. Shanks may be pre-cooked, then grilled

A boned leg of lamb may be spread flat and barbecued like a steak. Marinate in red wine mixture, then cook over medium coals. During cooking, brush often with same mixture used for marinating

Split Leg of Lamb

    1 leg of lamb (about 5 pounds)

Marinade:

    2 cups dry red table wine   3 cloves peeled garlic
    2 teaspoons salt   Pepper to taste
    2 teaspoons poultry seasoning

Ask your meatman to bone the leg of lamb, being careful not to cut through the meat.

Spread out meat in shallow pan, and marinate 24 hours in above mixture. Barbecue the marinated lamb over medium hot coals, placing fat side up first to hold in the heat; turn meat with tongs. Brush meat often during barbecuing with same mixture used for marinating.

Meat will become medium rare (still slightly pink inside) in 45 minutes to 1 hour. When barbecued, the meat loses its ragged appearance, and the fat cooks away, leaving browned, crisp covering.

To carve meat, start at one end and cut ¼-inch-thick slices across the grain. Serves 6.

Split Loin Roast

This method gives not ordinary barbecued lamb chops, but delicious small "lamb roasts" for each guest. The meat selected is a split loin of lamb—preferably hung for 8 to 10 days at the market before barbecuing. Have the meatman divide the split loin into about 6 chops, cutting through the bone but not completely separating the cuts. In this way the whole large piece can be cooked as one roast, yet easily divided into large loin chops for serving.

Rub the meat lightly with a cut clove of garlic, then roast on the grill over glowing coals. Turn as frequently as necessary for even cooking, and baste with a favorite barbecue sauce or not, as desired. Ordinarily 40 to 45 minutes should be long enough to allow for the roasting. Then, with a sharp knife, divide into chops and allow one for each serving. Serves 6.

A half rack of lamb may be barbecued in the same way if you want to use the rib cut instead of the loin.

PORK

Barbecued Canned Ham

Start the fire 3 hours before you eat. Open the canned ham; place the can in a large kettle (or dishpan) and pour in enough water so it comes to within 2 inches of top of can. Cover the kettle with a lid or aluminum foil. Simmer until ham is heated through, about 1½ hours for an 8 to 12-pound ham.

Remove meat from the can and place on a grill over low coals. Baste occasionally with the following mixture as the ham cooks: ⅔ cup catsup, ¼ cup white distilled vinegar, 2 tablespoons brown sugar, and salt and pepper to taste. Turning every 15 minutes, barbecue ham until it is lightly browned and crusty, from 1 to 1½ hours.

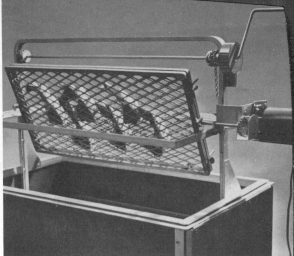

Bacon cooks quickly and evenly on this collapsible grill which has aluminum foil under the charcoal to reflect heat

A revolving grill provides even heat for cooking chops. With each turn of grill, chops are self-basted with own juices

Grilled Bacon

The best results are obtained by buying part of a side of bacon and having it sliced somewhat thicker than is customary. If there is a large crowd, the bacon should be first sliced and then replaced in its original block form and put into a bread pan. This is placed in the oven for 15 minutes at medium heat. In that way much of the surplus fat is removed, which reduces the possibility of flare-ups in cooking the bacon. Then place the bacon strips, separated, on the grill over a slow fire and cook, turning once or twice, until done.

Spicy Spareribs

2 pounds spareribs	2 dashes Tabasco
1 can (8 oz.) tomato sauce	1 tablespoon steak sauce
4 whole cloves	2 tablespoons vinegar
1/8 cinnamon stick	1 tablespoon sugar
1 stalk celery, chopped fine (or	1/2 teaspoon chili powder
1/4 teaspoon celery salt)	2 tablespoons chutney
1 clove garlic (or	1/8 teaspoon dry mustard
1/4 teaspoon garlic salt)	1 small onion, chopped fine

Leave ribs in one piece. Cook all other ingredients for 20 minutes or until blended to taste. Baste ribs frequently with this sauce during barbecuing. Serves 2.

Meal is broiled in skillets on three flowerpot "hibachis." Pots are first lined with foil, then partially filled with sand, and then fired with the charcoal

Smoky Spareribs

3 pounds pork spareribs	Pinch each of rosemary
Liquid smoke	leaves, ginger, and
1 clove garlic	coarsely ground black
1 onion	pepper
Few sprigs parsley	½ cup dry sherry
Salt	2 tablespoons tomato paste
	2 tablespoons sugar

Cut ribs into serving pieces and swab generously with liquid smoke. Place in a shallow open baking pan. Chop garlic, onion, and parsley together until fine; toss over meat. Sprinkle with salt, rosemary leaves, ginger, and pepper. Cover pan with waxed paper and let stand overnight.

When ready to cook, remove from pan and grill over a slow fire. Mix sherry, tomato paste, and sugar, and use for basting sauce. Grill until ribs are well browned and meat is tender, basting frequently with sauce. Serves 3 to 4.

Grilled Pork Chops

Take thick pork chops—soak for at least one hour (completely submerged) in juice from canned pears. Charcoal barbecue until well done.

Roasted Savory Spareribs

Select as many sides of spareribs as required and have the meatman crack them down the middle. Cut between the ribs into serving-size pieces. Rub each piece well with a mixture of 2 tablespoons rubbed sage to 1 cup flour.

Place the ribs over charcoal fire and cook slowly for 45 minutes to 1 hour, depending on the thickness of the ribs and the heat of the fire. Turn frequently and swab often with a sauce made by combining the following ingredients.

Sauce:

1 teaspoon garlic salt	1 teaspoon dry mustard
1 teaspoon onion salt	1/2 cup olive oil
1/2 teaspoon freshly ground pepper	1/2 cup vinegar
1 teaspoon seasoned salt	1 1/2 cups cold water

Spareribs with Onion

Sweet onions, chopped fine	Salt and pepper
Pork spareribs, cracked	Butter to sauté onions

Spread finely chopped onions on spareribs, roll up with onions inside and place in refrigerator or cooler overnight. Just before barbecuing, scrape off onions and season meat with salt and freshly ground pepper. Sauté onions in butter and serve with spareribs. No barbecue sauce required.

Chef's Spareribs

1/4 cup brown sugar	2 to 3 pounds pork spareribs
1 tablespoon salt	1/4 cup vinegar
1 tablespoon celery seed	1 cup canned tomato sauce
1 tablespoon chili powder	or purée
1 teaspoon paprika	

Mix the dry ingredients and rub part of the mixture into the ribs. Combine remainder of mixture with the vinegar and tomato sauce for basting. Let ribs stand an hour or longer, if convenient, then spread on grill over slow fire, basting occasionally with sauce. To reduce cooking time, pre-cook ribs in kitchen oven until almost tender, then finish on barbecue grill. Serves 3 or 4.

Easy Rib Barbecue

Select meaty pork spareribs or lamb breast and cut in pieces. Place between wire toaster. Cook about 5 inches above bed of coals. Grill for 25 minutes, turning every 5 minutes, then brush with barbecue sauce and continue grilling for 10 to 15 minutes longer. Ribs may also be conveniently cooked in a revolving grill or on a spit.

Seasoned Spareribs

5 pounds spareribs	1/4 cup wine vinegar
1 teaspoon salt	1/4 cup Worcestershire
1/8 teaspoon pepper	1 cup catsup
1 lemon, sliced thin	2 cups hot water
1/2 cup minced onions	1/4 cup brown sugar
1 teaspoon chili powder	Dash of Tabasco
1 teaspoon celery salt	1 ginger root sliced thin

Place spareribs on grill rounded side up, sprinkle with salt and pepper, arrange lemon slices over ribs. Baste with sauce made of remaining ingredients. Serves 6.

Spareribs Encino

Cut 6 pounds lean pork spareribs into individual-sized servings. Broil over coals in barbecue, until golden brown. Brush with barbecue sauce (see below). Place in covered roasting pan and let steam on back of the barbecue grill for at least one hour. Do not allow ribs to dry out. Baste frequently with sauce and fat from bottom of roaster. Serves 6.

Sauce:

2 large onions, minced	1 pinch each sage, oregano, thyme, rosemary, sweet basil
2 tablespoons olive oil	
8 large, ripe tomatoes	Salt and pepper to taste
1 green pepper, sliced	2 tablespoons white wine vinegar
1/4 cup chopped celery leaves	Sherry wine

In a large saucepan, sauté onions in olive oil until transparent. Quarter tomatoes and add to onions with green pepper, celery leaves, herbs, salt, and pepper. Cover and simmer slowly until tomatoes are soft. Put mixture through a coarse sieve to remove tomato seeds and other solids. Return mixture to stove, add vinegar, and let simmer to a thick paste, stirring frequently. When ready to use, dilute with ¾ cup sherry to ½ cup of barbecue paste. The paste may be made ahead in quantities and sealed in jars or bottles.

Barbemush Appetizer

1 pound salt pork, diced	½ teaspoon oregano
3 or 4 large onions, minced	½ teaspoon cumin seed
1 clove garlic, minced	2½ cups yellow cornmeal
4 cups water	¼ cup sliced green olives
1 tablespoon chili powder	

The day before the barbecue, fry the salt pork slowly until crisp; sauté onions and garlic in the drippings until golden; set aside.

Put water in the top part of a double boiler and bring to a boil; add seasonings and gradually stir in the cornmeal; cover and cook over boiling water for about 45 minutes. When done, add salt pork, onions, and olives. Turn out into a well-greased square pan that will give ample slices. Let stand until the next day.

An hour before barbecuing meat, grill well-oiled ½-inch slices of the cold mush over a fairly hot fire. The slices will lose moisture and shrink, and when thoroughly done and crisp, will let go of the grill so they can be turned easily. Cook till crisp, and if slightly scorched, so much the better. Tier them up on the side of the grill while cooking the meat.

Perro Con Queso

Here's a novel way to cook the ever-faithful hot dog: Take any quantity of frankfurters (the short, chubby ones are best) and core them with a piece of thin-wall, ⅜-inch copper tubing, that has been sharpened at the cutting end. Cut strips of cheese ⅜-inch square, and stuff in the hole. Grill until the frank is cooked and the cheese melted inside. Serve in toasted hot dog rolls. The frankfurter cores have to be punched out of the tubing with a stick. Chop them up and add them to a fresh garden salad.

Poor Man's Barbecued Ham Slices

1 tablespoon dry mustard	Ham slices, cut 1/4 to 3/8 inch
1/2 tablespoon powdered ginger	thick (as many as you
1 cup spiced peach syrup (or	want)
any spiced fruit syrup)	

Make a paste of the dry mustard and ginger by adding the syrup slowly. Stir until a smooth sauce results.

Trim most of the fat from the ham slices and paint on one side with the sauce. Place on the grate, sauce side down, about 12 inches above a slow charcoal fire. Paint the top side of the ham. Turn the ham often and keep moist with the sauce.

Don't be in a hurry! Keep over slow fire for at lease 30 to 40 minutes. Don't let the slices rest on one side too long. Turn them often, let them brown, not burn, and use all of the sauce.

Charcoal Broiled Ham Steaks

1 slice tenderized ham,	1/2 cup juice from a can of
1/2 to 3/4 inch thick	sliced pineapple
3 teaspoons dry mustard	2 to 3 slices canned pineapple
1 cup brown sugar	

Put steaks on grill and baste with a thin paste of the mustard, brown sugar, and pineapple juice. Use mustard sparingly at first, then add more to taste. Remove steaks when brown. Put pineapple rings on grill and when they are a steaming brown, serve them on top of the steaks.

Serve with baked candied yams, hot rolls, and a salad of mixed greens. Serves 2 or 3.

Ham With Pineapple Sauce

Broil thin slices of ham on the grill. When slightly brown, begin basting with pineapple sauce and continue until ham is tender and well seasoned.

Basting sauce:

1 cup brown sugar	2 tablespoons dry mustard
1/2 cup vinegar	1 cup pineapple juice

Cook the sugar, vinegar, and mustard together slowly for 3 minutes. Remove from the heat and add the pineapple juice.

FOWL

Barbecued Broilers

Use young chickens weighing 1½ to 2 pounds. Have them cleaned at the market, and split for broiling. Broil halves on the grill over a bed of coals, placing cavity side down first, skin side last. Baste frequently.

Basting sauce:

2/3 cup butter
2/3 cup hot water
  2 teaspoons A-1 sauce
1½ tablespoons lemon juice
  ¼ teaspoon Tabasco

2 teaspoons sugar
1 teaspoon salt
  A few grains cayenne
2 teaspoons flour

Melt the butter and add the water and other liquids. Blend the dry ingredients and stir into the liquid, stirring well. Cook for 2 or 3 minutes or until the mixture thickens slightly.

Some cooks prefer to soak chickens in California olive oil, with a liberal seasoning of coarsely ground black pepper, for 4 or 5 hours before barbecuing in this way.

Ranch Style Chicken

Cut 3 frying chickens into pieces as for frying. Brush with melted butter, and place over coals for about 5 minutes to sear, and then turn. Brush with sauce and turn every 3 to 5 minutes, brushing with sauce at each turn. Time required is about 45 minutes. Serves 6.

Basting sauce:

½ cup white apple vinegar
1/3 cup salad oil
1½ teaspoons Worcestershire
½ teaspoon minced onion
1 clove garlic, minced

3 teaspoons salt
1 teaspoon paprika
1½ teaspoons tomato paste
6 to 8 drops Tabasco
¼ teaspoon dry mustard

Best to make the sauce at least 24 hours before using.

Chicken often gives off a great deal of smoke when broiled over charcoal, but may be cooked indoors if draft is good

Put chicken halves on grill first with hollow side down. Then do final cooking with hollow side up to hold juices

Barbecued Chicken, Paprika

2 fryers or broilers (about 1½ to 2 pounds each)
2 cups olive oil

2 or 3 cloves garlic, well minced
4 heaping tablespoons paprika
Salt and pepper

Quarter chicken, wash quickly, and dry well; place in shallow pan. Mix together the oil, garlic, and paprika, then pour over chicken. Marinate for 3 or 4 hours, turning the chicken about every half hour. Season with salt and pepper and place quarters on grill. Broil over hot coals, baste frequently with the marinade. Serves 4.

Turkey Steaks

Here's a recipe that will leave your meatman shaking his head in disbelief and will stir your guests into pelting you with questions:

Buy a large, hard-frozen, eviscerated tom turkey—the bigger the better. Have your meatman cut it on his power saw into 1-inch transverse slices, starting at the front of the breastbone, and working back to about where the thighs join the body. If you're serving a large number of people, have him cut more slices—one slice will make two good servings. The two ends that are left can be kept frozen until you need them.

Chicken suspended alongside coals in combination vertical-horizontal grill roasts to a golden brown without smoking. Drippings fall into pan below instead of on coals, may be spooned back on bird as baste or collected for use in gravy. Rotating device in brass cylinder keeps bird turning before coals

Now lay the frozen slices out in a large flat pan (you can stack them) and drizzle on enough cooking oil to coat each one. As the slices thaw, the oil and juices will make a fine marinade in the pan. This should be brushed back over the slices from time to time. When they are completely thawed, divide each slice into two steaks with a sharp, heavy knife. (You'll find that the cross-sections of breast and backbone will split easily.)

Have a good, hot bed of coals going in the barbecue. Arrange the steaks in toasting racks, brush with basting sauce (¼ pound butter, ½ cup dry white wine, salt, and pepper). Broil about 8 inches from the fire for around 10 minutes on each side. Turn them a couple of times during the cooking, and brush with more butter-wine mixture.

Serve them up, one to a person, with the remainder of the basting sauce heated and spooned over each serving, and have the guests guess what they're eating. You'll get quite a variety of answers—from pork, veal, to swordfish. The steaks don't taste like the customary roast turkey, but you'll agree that it is some of the best turkey you ever sank a tooth into. Once again, not too much cooking. Don't let them dry out.

Grilled Young Turkey

1 6 to 9-pound broiling turkey
Salt and pepper
1 cup favorite barbecue sauce

Dash liquid smoke
Melted butter

Cut turkey in pieces as you would a frying chicken and lay in roasting pan. Sprinkle lightly with salt and pepper, and cover with barbecue sauce to which liquid smoke has been added. Marinate at least 5 hours, or overnight.

Split skin of turkey and rub sauce under it on meat, but do not remove skin. Grill turkey over charcoal coals, turning pieces frequently, and painting pieces with pastry brush dipped in melted butter. Cooking time, approximately 45 minutes. Serves 6 to 8.

Broiled Split Turkey

Split a 5 or 6-pound young turkey down the back and remove breastbone so it can flatten out like a thick steak. Have at hand a bowl of melted butter, mixed with a little chopped garlic and parsley. Broil the turkey like a steak over a deep bed of coals. Baste liberally with the melted butter.

Keep a bowl of water at hand. When flames spring up, sprinkle water (don't splash) on flames. By sprinkling lightly you create little steam clouds. After 45 minutes of this alternate steaming and broiling with frequent turnings you will have a broiled fowl that tastes the way pheasant is supposed to taste, and often doesn't.

Wild Ducks—Grilled

Clean the ducks, wipe well, and split down the back. Season with salt and pepper, rub with fine olive oil and place on the grill. Let them cook from 7 to 10 minutes on each side, turning them over at least twice. A wild duck should never be cooked dry. Most chefs think it should just reach the point where the blood will not run if the flesh is pierced with fork in carving.

Place on a very hot dish and pour over them melted butter which has been mixed with lemon juice and minced parsley. Garnish with watercress or parsley sprigs.

Well-Barbecued Wild Duck

1 cup olive oil	1 tablespoon celery seeds
1/2 cup vinegar	1 teaspoon salt
1/4 cup soy	1/4 teaspoon pepper (or to taste)
6 cloves garlic, mashed	4 pintails (or other wild ducks)
1 sprig rosemary	

Combine all sauce ingredients and simmer 10 minutes to blend flavors. Cut duck into halves and barbecue, turning several times and swabbing sauce on generously. Forty-five minutes over a rather hot fire should do the trick if you like yours "medium." Cut the time for those characters who want their birds still kicking. Serves 8.

Broiled Wild Mallard Duck

1 mallard duck (2 to 3 1/2 pounds)	2 teaspoons Worcestershire
1 cup prepared French dressing	2 teaspoons grated orange peel
1 teaspoon dry mustard	1 teaspoon grated lemon peel

Split duck up backbone with poultry shears. Place breast side down on meat cutting board and break down breast bones by pressing with another board or by pounding gently with a meat tenderizing mallet.

Mix the sauce ingredients together and use mixture to baste the duck liberally. Insert the duck in a hinged wire grill and broil over hot coals until done to taste, basting it at least once more while cooking. We recommend not over 10 minutes a side; most duck fanciers prefer 5 minutes a side. Divide duck at breastbone into two portions and serve. Serves 2.

Small, whole broilers split down back and flattened out for broiling on grill. Barbecue, set in fireplace, is a Chinese wok with legs made of long bolts, threaded into nuts welded to bowl. The grill is made of disc of expanded metal

Pheasant

Halve or quarter the bird, then marinate pieces in a mixture of half olive oil and half white wine. Sprinkle drained sections with paprika just before cooking. Broil on the grill, basting often with the oil-wine mixture. Add a little sprinkle of salt before serving. The oil-wine blend is used for basting because it does not dominate the natural flavor of the pheasant. Serves 4.

Quail

Clean and wipe the birds well. Cut them through the back and spread. Rub them with melted butter and season with salt and freshly ground pepper to taste. Fasten a strip of bacon to breast of each bird with skewers. Place on the grill and cook for 15 or 20 minutes, according to size. Cook breast side up. Serve on buttered toast, allowing a slice for each bird.

Chinese Barbecued Duck

2 or 3 young ducks, quartered	1 teaspoon grated fresh ginger
1 cup sherry	(or powdered)
1/3 cup honey or brown sugar	1 teaspoon dry mustard
1 tablespoon soy sauce	Sesame seeds

Select lean, meaty young ducks. Trim off all excess fat possible. Pour marinade made of sherry, honey, soy sauce, ginger, and mustard over quartered duck and let stand several hours, or overnight, in refrigerator. Place on grill over bed of coals and barbecue until done, about ¾ hour.

Baste duck with remaining marinade during cooking. Sprinkle with sesame seeds before serving. Serves 6 to 8.

Squab

Split squab down the back. Brush with soy sauce; barbecue 20 to 25 minutes, turning and basting occasionally with mixture of soy sauce and melted butter.

FISH/SEAFOOD

Mackerel

Clean, cut off the head, and dry with a damp cloth; do not wash. Split open and flatten out. Soak in a solution of salt and water (plenty of salt) for 24 hours. Then wash off all traces of salt and paint liberally with liquid smoke. Grill lightly for 5 minutes to a side over oak bark coals. Serve hot or cold. Makes a good snack, or even a meal with salad and beer.

Trout

Trout, when wrapped in bacon, fastened with a skewer, and cooked on the barbecue grill is a dish fit for the gods. Cook over glowing coals in a hinged, double rack, and by the time the bacon is cooked crisp, the fish is done also.

Trout grilled with corn. Trout cleaned, wrapped in corn husks and placed right on coals. Husked corn basted with butter-oil mixture while trout cook. Rotate corn, trout. Grill 20 minutes

Grill with hood can double as oven for baking. With hood turned down, first bake potatoes on the grill. Then keep them hot on the warming shelf while you cook trout and corn on opened grill

Prawns

1 pound raw (green) prawns	1/2 teaspoon freshly ground pepper
1/2 cup dark molasses	
1 can (8 oz.) Spanish-style tomato sauce	1 teaspoon dry mustard
	1/4 teaspoon Tabasco
1/2 teaspoon salt	Pinch of thyme
	1/4 cup salad or olive oil

Wash, shuck, and clean raw prawns. Toss into boiling salted water, reduce heat, and simmer for 15 minutes. Drain and cool, but do not rinse as this tends to toughen them.

Mix all the rest of the ingredients together to make the sauce. If you do not like too hot a mixture, cut down on the pepper, mustard, and Tabasco. Add the cooked prawns and turn in the sauce until completely covered.

Scoop out the prawns and arrange on the barbecue grill or thread on skewers. Cook over hot coals. Turn prawns two or three times and baste frequently with the sauce left in the bowl. Serve hot, right from the grill. This is finger food, so have plenty of napkins nearby.

Pickled prawns make good appetizers served as is or with a sauce. Simmer them in a mixture of half wine vinegar and half water that has been seasoned with pickling spices, curry powder, onion, and a couple of cloves of garlic. These should not be drained but should chill right in the pickling liquid. Serves 4 as appetizers, 2 as main course.

Tabangas Baked Fish

Select a good 5 to 7-pound salmon, striped bass, or steelhead. Clean, leaving head and tail intact. Stuff with this dressing:

2 cups chopped tomatoes	Soy sauce to taste
1/2 cup chopped onions	Lemon juice to taste
1 teaspoon ginger	Dash of Tabasco
1 teaspoon salt	Little minced garlic

Fasten edges of fish together with skewers or toothpicks, and wrap whole fish in greased butcher paper or a large sweet leaf, such as banana. Bake over charcoal fire for about 2 hours. Serves 6 to 8.

Lobster tails broil on grill as potato
patties brown in skillet. Broil lobster
with shell side down until shell browns,
then turn and brown meaty side. Baste
frequently with melted butter or oil

Jack smelt, tomatoes steam together in
seaweed. Rub cleaned fish with oil, salt,
and pepper; top with tomato slices;
wrap in seaweed. Place over low coals,
cover with dishpan, steam 45 minutes

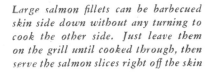

Large salmon fillets can be barbecued
skin side down without any turning to
cook the other side. Just leave them
on the grill until cooked through, then
serve the salmon slices right off the skin

Celestial Shrimp

These shrimp are broiled in the shell, so serve them with plenty of enormous paper napkins or, in the Chinese manner, with hot, wet towels.

Select 2 pounds of jumbo green (uncooked) prawns; slit the backs with a pair of pointed scissors, then wash out the sand veins.

Marinate the prawns for 2 hours in the following mixture: ½ cup *each* of soy, salad oil, and sherry to which you have added a tablespoon of minced green or crystallized ginger.

Drain the prawns, put in a fine-meshed hinged broiler, and cook over coals for 3 minutes; turn and cook 2 or 3 more minutes, or until the shells are pinkly browned. Serve immediately. You'll have 30 to 40 prawns.

Oysters in Bacon Wrap

Season oysters with salt and pepper, and wrap each oyster in a thin strip of bacon and secure the wrapping with wooden toothpicks. Arrange the "blanketed" oysters in a hinged, double, wire rack. Barbecue quickly over a hot bed of coals, turning often. As soon as the bacon has "sizzled" to your fancy, your barbecued oysters are done.

Serve with sliced lemon, a little drawn butter, A-1 sauce and Tabasco, not forgetting, of course, a cold bottle of sauterne or hock, the natural accompaniments of oysters.

Grilled Salmon

Clean fish and remove heads. Flatten out in a triangular shape by completely splitting the fish through the tails and pressing them. Layer them in rock salt overnight. Rinse well with cold water and dry; place in hinged wire grill frame or in rack improvised from chicken wire. Broil flesh side down for 1½ hours, then expose other side. Total cooking time about 2½ to 3 hours. For fuel, use alderwood, damp and green, to assure plenty of smoke.

Variation:

Fill body cavity of cleaned salmon with chopped onions, parsley, and salt; place fish on square of chicken wire, fold over and hook loose ends, and place on grill. When cooked, the skin will adhere to the chicken wire, which is discarded.

Broiled Salmon Steaks

An application of lemon juice adds greatly to the flavor of broiled salmon steaks. About an hour before cooking, brush both sides of each steak with lemon juice, cover loosely with waxed paper, and place in the refrigerator. When ready to cook, dust with flour, salt, and pepper. Then place on the grill.

Bass and Sausage

For a novelty, stuff bass with Mexican sausage, and grill over the coals. Type of sausage used is known as "chorizo."

Lobster

Kill lobster by inserting knife in back between body and tail shells. Split lengthwise and clean. Wash and dry carefully. Brush meat with melted butter or oil. Dust with salt and pepper. Broil (shell side down) until shell browns. Turn over and brown meaty side. Baste frequently with butter or oil. Serve with melted butter and lemon juice.

Barbecued Crab

Clean cooked crabs; crack legs and break body into 2 or 3 pieces. Place in baking pan or individual serving casseroles, cover with sauce (recipe on page 128), and heat over coals for about 20 minutes or until hot. Pour sauce over hot crab, and serve.

Sauce may also be served in separate bowl for dunking. To garnish individual servings, place a large crab claw in center of the casserole with a stuffed olive or tomato or lime wedge grasped in the claw.

Charcoal-Broiled Kidneys

Beef, veal, lamb, and pork kidneys may all be successfully cooked over charcoal. Split the kidneys and remove cores; brush with oil or melted butter, seasoned, if you wish, with garlic or with bacon drippings. Broil over a medium hot fire, but not too long or they will toughen. The kidneys will take from 5 to 15 minutes to cook, depending on size. They are done when brown on the outside but still jucily pink inside. Slice kidneys and serve with melted butter.

Kidneys may also be cut in pieces, wrapped in bacon, and charcoal-broiled. In this case it is not necessary to brush them with oil. Cook until bacon is very crisp. Serve with broiled tomatoes or, if desired, as part of a mixed grill with broiled sausage and lamb chops or liver.

Charcoal-Broiled Liver

Liver is at its best when cooked over charcoal. Use beef, veal, or lamb liver, and have it sliced at least 1 inch thick. Brush well with melted butter, oil, or bacon drippings. Broil over a medium hot fire, allowing the meat to become crisply brown on the outside but not dry in the middle. Most persons prefer liver broiled medium rare (make a slit in the meat with a sharp knife to see degree of doneness). Serve with bacon and fried onions, or broiled tomatoes, or eggplant.

Charcoal-Broiled Pigs Feet

The pigs feet must be boiled before they are grilled. Cook them, whole or split, in water to cover, with salt, an onion, and an herb bouquet. Simmer until tender—from 3 to 4 hours. Drain, brush well with softened butter, then roll in crumbs. Broil until nicely browned on all sides. Serve with charcoal-roasted potatoes and with sauerkraut heated in a pot at the back of the grill.

Broiled Brains

Beef, veal, or lamb brains may be broiled over charcoal. A beef brain serves three, a veal brain serves two, and a lamb brain serves one. Unless you are a master at fire control and charcoal cookery, we think it is best to parboil the brains first. Soak brains in cold water, then simmer for 15 minutes in water to cover. (Add 1 tablespoon lemon juice and 1 teaspoon salt to each quart of water.) Drain, and cover with ice water; remove discolored spots. Split brains and dip in melted butter, then roll in fine crumbs.

Broil over a slow charcoal fire, turning so that both sides will brown. Baste with a little more butter while cooking. The brains will broil in about 10 minutes. Serve them with lemon wedges, crisp bacon, and drawn butter or tartar sauce.

Charcoal-Broiled Sweetbreads

You cook these exactly the same way you do brains (see directions above). Or they may be parboiled, cut in pieces, and threaded on skewers, alternated with mushroom caps. Dip filled skewers in melted butter and broil until nicely browned.

Broiled Beef Heart

If you like rare beef, you will like beef heart sliced ½ inch thick and broiled quickly over charcoal. The slices should first be marinated in equal parts wine and olive oil, or in melted butter. If cooked lightly, the heart will be tender. Do not attempt this method if you like your beef well done, for longer broiling will make the beef heart tough.

Charcoal-Broiled Tripe

Like tongue, tripe needs pre-cooking until fork-tender. Do it in a pressure cooker or by boiling in salted water. Cut in strips, dip in melted butter, and broil on both sides until brown. Serve with individual dishes of melted butter and with wedges of lemon. Fried onions and green pepper, and charcoal-roasted potatoes go well with this.

Charcoal-Broiled Short Ribs

Have beef short ribs separated but left long. Marinate for 24 to 48 hours in a mixture of ½ cup salad oil, ½ cup soy, 2 cloves crushed garlic, 2 teaspoons sugar, and 3 tablespoons crushed sesame seeds. Broil the ribs slowly until crisp and brown and tender to the fork; this will take from 30 to 60 minutes.

FRUITS/VEGETABLES

A hinged grill with narrow grids is the best way to handle the broiling of fruits and vegetables. They usually require brushing with butter or basting during the cooking.

Fruits

Apples. Cut unpeeled apples in thick slices and dip in butter. Broil on both sides, sprinkling with cinnamon and sugar toward the end of the cooking.

Bananas. Peel bananas and cut in half. Wrap with bacon and broil on both sides. Or use unpeeled bananas and make a slit about 3 inches long in the skin. Force 1 tablespoon of honey into this opening and let stand for ½ hour. Place on grill and cook for about 8 minutes, turning frequently.

Dates. Remove pits, stuff with Cheddar cheese, wrap in bacon, and broil. These are for an appetizer.

Figs. Wrap fresh figs in bacon and broil until bacon is crisp.

Grapefruit. Cut grapefruit in halves and remove seeds. Loosen segments from the skin and section membranes. Cover with brown or white sugar to start the juice running, and after half an hour, add more sugar, if desired. Dot tops with butter, pour about a tablespoon of sherry or rum over each half. Place on grill and broil until fruit is thoroughly heated.

Oranges. Cut unpeeled oranges in thick slices, dip in melted butter, then dust lightly with flour. Broil on both sides.

Peaches. Use fresh or canned peaches. If fresh, they should be peeled and halved. Brush with butter and broil, cut side down, until brown, then turn and fill cavities with butter and brown sugar, and continue broiling until brown on the bottom. If desired, put a little sherry or rum in the cavities and serve them as a dessert with cold sour cream or ice cream.

Pears. Do these in the manner suggested for peaches.

Pineapple. Cut a fresh pineapple of average size lengthwise into 8 sections. Place in baking pan and drip honey—about a tablespoon to a section—over the fruit. Let stand for ½ hour and then grill. Or, use sliced pineapple, either canned or fresh, and brush with melted butter before broiling on both sides.

Vegetables

Artichokes. Use cooked artichoke bottoms, and marinate them in French dressing before broiling.

Carrots. Cook unpeeled carrots until just tender, peel, dip in butter, and broil.

Corn. There are many ways to cook corn on the cob over a charcoal fire, and these are just a few of the variations:

1. Use unhusked ears. Lay back husks and remove silk. Return husks to former position and wire into place (with any fine wire) at center and near tip of cob, covering the kernels as well as possible. Roast on the grill, turning 3 or 4 times so that all surfaces are exposed to the heat. Snip the wires with wire cutter, husk the ears (gloves are necessary), and serve.

2. Open husk at one end; let about 2 tablespoons of barbecue sauce run inside the ear. Smooth husk back in place; tie and cook as above.

3. Pull husks back, remove silk, brush corn generously with garlic butter. Replace husks and place ears on grill. Dip a clean burlap sack in warm water, wring it out slightly, and place it over the ears so that they will steam. Let the ears grill 5 minutes on one side. Remove burlap, turn ears, re-cover with burlap, sprinkling it with more water. Grill 5 minutes longer.

4. Strip ears down to last 3 or 4 husks and place in ice water 30 minutes or longer. Drain well and place on grill for only 15

This is one of several ways to roast corn over a charcoal fire. Pull back husks and strip off silk. Brush kernels with seasoned butter; replace husks; tie ends

Cover corn with damp burlap; steam on grill for 5 minutes. Remove burlap, turn ears, dampen burlap, and put it back over corn. Grill 5 minutes longer

or 20 minutes. Delicious with lots of melted butter and salt!

5. Husk corn, wrap in bacon, and broil until bacon is crisp and the exposed corn brown.

Eggplant. Cut unpeeled eggplant in slices or wedges. Marinate for an hour in garlic-seasoned olive oil, and broil until nicely browned, brushing with more oil during the cooking.

Mushrooms. Select large ones, remove stems, and dip caps in butter. Put in a hinged broiler and cook stem side down, then turn, fill cavities with butter (seasoned with tarragon, chives, or dill, if desired), and finish broiling. Serve as an appetizer, or serve with any meat, shellfish, or poultry.

Onions. Take big whole yellow onions just the way they come from the grocery, leave the dry outside skins on, wet them thoroughly, and place them on the grill. Roll them around while you're cooking steaks, spareribs, or whatever. By the time everything else is done, they'll be black on the outside and soft and creamy inside.

Peppers. Cut green peppers in quarters, remove seeds, and dip in olive oil before broiling.

Tomatoes. Cut firm tomatoes in halves, brush with butter, sprinkle with salt and pepper, and broil, cut side down. When

To grill husked ears of corn, place over slow heat for about 20 minutes. Rotate ears and baste frequently with a mixture of equal parts butter and oil

Another method of roasting corn in the husks: Pull down husks, remove silk, wrap with bacon. Rearrange husks, tie at top. Grill 20 minutes, turning often

brown, turn, brush with more butter, and continue cooking until barely tender. If desired, buttered toast crumbs may be sprinkled on the cut sides after turning.

Foil-Wrapped Fruits and Vegetables

Many fruits and vegetables may be cooked in this manner. They are first peeled and cut in slices. Put them on squares of heavy foil, season, seal, and cook on the grill until tender. Turn during the cooking. Test for doneness by piercing through the foil.

Compared to the other methods of charcoal cooking, this one makes serving and eating easy, but the foods do not have the smoky flavor of those exposed to the charcoal. They taste very much like foods cooked in the kitchen.

Fruits

Apples. Peel and slice; season with butter and sugar and with cinnamon, coriander, or mace. Wrap in foil and broil until fork tender.

Bananas. Peel and slice or quarter; season with sugar and butter; wrap in foil and broil.

Oranges. Peel oranges and divide into segments. Season with butter, sugar, and cinnamon or rosemary. Wrap and broil.

Peaches. Peel and cut in slices. Season with butter and brown sugar. Wrap and then broil.

Pears. Peel and slice; season with butter, sugar, and ginger, or add slivered candied ginger. Wrap and broil.

Pineapple. Use pineapple chunks. Season with butter and sugar. Wrap and broil.

The fruits may be served with grilled meats, or as a dessert.

Vegetables

Shredded peeled beets, sliced carrots, corn cut from the cob, sliced peeled eggplant, sliced mushrooms, sliced onions, sliced green peppers, sliced or diced white or sweet potatoes, shelled peas, and sliced squash may all be foil-wrapped and cooked on the grill. Season them with plenty of butter and with salt and pepper before wrapping. If desired, vegetables may also be cooked in combinations. Onions and potatoes, corn and green pepper, and peas and mushrooms are good together. Serve the vegetables with meats or fish from the grill.

Baked Potatoes

If you have no built-in oven, and dislike baking potatoes in ashes, use an inexpensive sheet-iron oven designed for use over a gas burner. Set it over a corner of the grill and the potatoes will be baked beautifully without charred skins.

Another way to bake potatoes is to place the scrubbed potatoes, rubbed well with bacon drippings or butter, on a wire rack which holds them up about ⅜ of an inch above a flat plate. Then cover them with a roaster lid. Baked this way, they must be turned and moved frequently, to prevent over-charring of the skin. To serve, wipe the skins with a clean cloth, slightly mash the ends toward the middle, cut open and put butter in the hole. Butter which has been softened, mixed with chopped chives and then chilled firm again, is especially good in barbecue-baked potatoes.

Roasting on the spit

Spit roasting is the oldest form of cooking, and many experts still consider it the best. Actually, it is the only *true* roasting, for foods cooked in the oven are really baked.

The superior flavor and extra juiciness of spit-cooked meats are unquestioned, for the meats are self-basted with their own juices while turning, and the only loss is that of excess fat. Spit cooking has another big advantage in that it needs little supervision once the meat is properly spitted over a well-built fire.

Trussing and Balancing

Unless the meat—or fish, or fowl—is correctly trussed and balanced, there will be trouble. The small electric motors with which spits are equipped are not powerful enough to offset the jerking and stopping caused by meat that is spitted off center. The motor may break down; and even if it doesn't, the food will be unevenly cooked.

Useful spit equipment: A) revolving basket; B) multiple double-pronged skewers; C) three styles of weight compensators; D) double holding fork; *E) double-pronged skewer; F) spit and holders; G) magnetized spit thermometer to indicate heat at level of rotating spit; and H) meat thermometer*

In all cases, the food should be as compact as possible. This means that it should be tied or trussed so that wings and legs of poultry will lie close to the body, and no small, oddly shaped pieces will protrude from the main mass of other meats.

Care must also be taken to assure that the meat will not slip around on the spit but will turn with it. This means that holding forks must be properly adjusted and tightened. In many cases, especially when several pieces of food are on one spit,

one or two extra skewers—long ones—must be inserted so that all will turn together.

The important thing in balancing is to have the spit pass through the center of gravity. This takes some experience; only way to judge the success of your effort is by eye and by the way the spitted meat comes to rest when you hold the ends of the spit in either hand or put it on props of equal height. Even when the meat is properly balanced at the beginning of the roasting period,

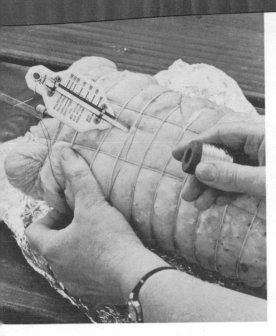

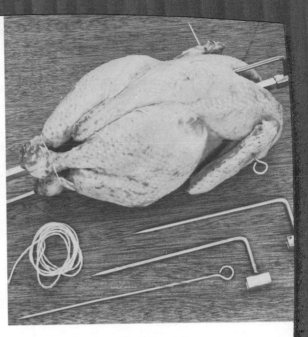

Insert meat thermometer into center of roll; do not touch end to spit. Use thin wire to hold thermometer to meat, spit

Chicken is shown ready for roasting. It is securely trussed and pinned. Cord, pin, special skewers used in preparation

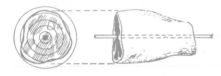

it may not remain that way. Sometimes more fat renders out from one part of the roast than from another. Several charcoal grills on the market today are equipped with a weight com-

Lamb legs, boned, tied, and balanced on the spit. Natural fat will baste meat, but extra baste is added for seasoning

Short ribs alternate with potatoes. Cut a small hole in center of potatoes before putting them on spit. Cook 1 hour

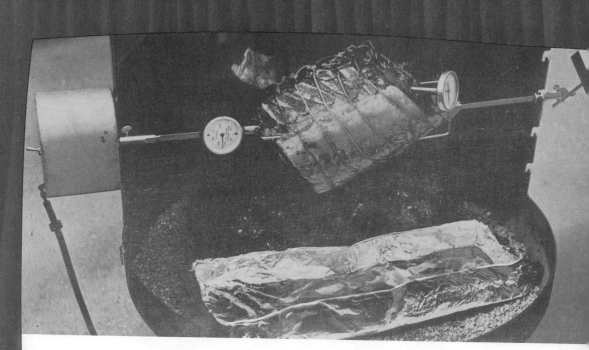

A 4-rib standing rib roast, spitted on the diagonal has a weight compensator at end of spit for balance. Magnetized *spit thermometer checks temperature of coals; meat thermometer is guide to doneness; foil pan catches fat drippings*

pensator. This makes balancing very easy. At least one such compensator can be adjusted while the cooking is actually in progress.

Fire and Direction of Turn

The fire for roasting should, generally speaking, be a little lower than that allowed for broiling. If a spit thermometer is used, it should read from 250° to 300°.

It is best to have the spit turn away from the cook when at the top of the turn (clockwise when you are facing the right end of the spit). The fat drops off on the upswing, not at the very bottom of the turn. If the spit turns away from you, you can catch dripping fat in a pan placed in front of the fire (the fire itself

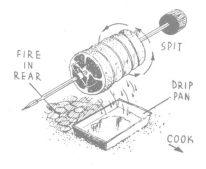

should be toward the back of the firebox). This arrangement prevents flaring, so that you may leave the roast unattended except for an occasional check of the fire.

If it is not feasible to have the spit turn in that direction, push the coals into a circle and put a pan in the center to catch drippings. This is less satisfactory because, as stated above, the drippings do not fall at the exact bottom of the turn.

Basting

A roast properly spitted and turning in the right direction will automatically baste itself with its own juices. If the spit turns evenly, as it will if well balanced, the meat will brown evenly too. We do not attempt here to suggest bastes for all the meats mentioned in this chapter, because most cooks have their own favorite ones. However, some are given here and there are more in the chapter on sauces and marinades.

We do want to point out, however, that unless the meat is very lean, basting is not really necessary.

Timing

Cooking time is bound to vary greatly for a number of reasons—size and temperature of the uncooked meat, temperature of the fire, temperature of the air, whether there is a wind, and, if so, whether the spit is shielded from it.

For all these reasons, it is most satisfactory to use a meat thermometer to determine when the meat has reached the degree of doneness desired.

The times suggested in this chapter are based on meats started at room temperature; remember that a large roast taken from the refrigerator will take 6 or 8 hours to reach that temperature.

One more point should be emphasized in regard to timing and temperature: All roasted meats, but particularly the larger ones, continue cooking after they are removed from the fire or the fire is doused. For this reason, the temperatures given here as a signal to end the cooking may increase from 5° to 10° by the time the meat is served. If the roast is allowed to turn on the spit after the fire is out, the juices will increase and carving will be easier.

Spit Roasting Time

Variety of Meat	Cut of Meat	Size or Weight	Warm-up Time for Frozen Meat		Recommended Heat of Fire*
			In Refrigerator to 40°	In Room 40° to 70°	
BEEF	Standing Rib	3 to 5 Ribs	36 to 40 Hrs.	8 Hrs.	Hot-Medium
	Rolled Rib	6 to 7 Pounds	36 to 40 Hrs.	8 Hrs.	Hot-Medium
	Spencer	8 to 10 Pounds	36 to 40 Hrs.	8 Hrs.	Hot-Medium
	Rump	3 to 5 Pounds	24 to 30 Hrs.	6 Hrs.	Medium
	Tenderloin (Whole)	4 to 6 Pounds	12 to 18 Hrs.	10 Hrs.	Hot
	Sirloin	5 to 7 Pounds	18 to 24 Hrs.	8 Hrs.	Hot-Medium
FISH	Large, Whole	10 to 20 Pounds	30 to 40 Hrs.	12 Hrs.	Slow
HAM	Smoked	We do not recommend roasting cured ham over charcoal. If you wish to			
LAMB	Leg	4 to 8 Pounds	15 to 40 Hrs.	5 to 7 Hrs.	Medium
	Rolled Shoulder	3 to 6 Pounds	15 to 30 Hrs.	4 to 6 Hrs.	Medium
	Saddle	6 to 16 Pounds	15 to 36 Hrs.	6 to 10 Hrs.	Medium
	Rack (Ribs)	4 to 7 Pounds	12 to 24 Hrs.	5 to 6 Hrs.	Medium
	Baby Lamb, Kid	12 to 25 Pounds	30 to 54 Hrs.	12 to 15 Hrs.	Medium
PORK	Loin	5 to 14 Pounds	28 to 36 Hrs.	6 to 10 Hrs.	Medium
	Shoulder	3 to 6 Pounds	24 to 30 Hrs.	6 to 8 Hrs.	Medium
	Fresh Ham	10 to 16 Pounds	30 to 48 Hrs.	10 to 15 Hrs.	Medium
	Spareribs	1½ to 3½ Pounds	4 to 7 Hrs.	2 to 3 Hrs.	Medium to Hot
	Suckling Pig	12 to 20 Pounds	30 to 54 Hrs.	12 to 15 Hrs.	Medium
POULTRY	Chicken	3 to 5 Pounds	10 to 12 Hrs.	4 to 5 Hrs.	Medium
	Cornish Hen	12 oz. to 1 Pound	8 to 11 Hrs.	2 to 3 Hrs.	Medium
	Squab	10 to 14 Ounces	8 to 11 Hrs.	2 to 3 Hrs.	Medium
	Turkey	10 to 25 Pounds	15 to 36 Hrs.	8 to 10 Hrs.	Medium
	Junior Goose	4 to 7 Pounds	13 to 20 Hrs.	5 to 7 Hrs.	Medium
	Goose	8 to 15 Pounds	20 to 30 Hrs.	6 to 9 Hrs.	Medium
	Duckling	4 to 6 Pounds	13 to 18 Hrs.	5 to 7 Hrs.	Medium
VEAL	Leg	8 to 14 Pounds	24 to 36 Hrs.	7 to 10 Hrs.	Medium
	Loin	10 to 13 Pounds	20 to 30 Hrs.	6 to 9 Hrs.	Medium
	Shoulder (Rolled)	3 to 5 Pounds	15 to 24 Hrs.	4 to 6 Hrs.	Medium
VENISON	Leg	9 to 12 Pounds	20 to 40 Hrs.	7 to 10 Hrs.	Hot-Medium
	Shoulder	5 to 7 Pounds	15 to 24 Hrs.	4 to 6 Hrs.	Hot-Medium
	Saddle	12 to 18 Pounds	18 to 40 Hrs.	8 to 12 Hrs.	Medium

* Hot fire, 325° or over; medium, 250 to 300°; slow, 150 to 225°. Check with thermometer.

Very Rare 120°-130°	Rare 130°-135°	Med.-rare 135°-145°	Medium 145°-155°	Well-done 155°-180°	
...½ to 2¼ Hrs.	1¾ to 2¼ Hrs.	2 to 2¾ Hrs.	2½ to 3 Hrs.	3 to 4½ Hrs.	1
...¼ to 2½ Hrs.	2 to 2¾ Hrs.	2¼ to 3 Hrs.	2¾ to 3¼ Hrs.	3¼ to 5 Hrs.	1
...½ to 2½ Hrs.	2½ to 3 Hrs.	2¾ to 3½ Hrs.	3 to 4 Hrs.	3½ to 5½ Hrs.	1
...¼ to 1¾ Hrs.	1½ to 2 Hrs.	1¾ to 2½ Hrs.	2½ to 3 Hrs.	3 to 4½ Hrs.	
25 to 40 Min.	35 to 45 Min.	45 to 60 Min.	50 Min. to 1¼ Hrs.	1 to 2 Hrs.	2
...1 to 1½ Hrs.	1¼ to 1¾ Hrs.	1¾ to 2¼ Hrs.	2¼ to 3 Hrs.	3 to 4 Hrs.	3
Cook to 135° or 140° internal temperature.					4
..., follow timing for fresh ham (below).					
60 to 65 Min.	1 to 1¼ Hrs.	1¼ to 1½ Hrs.	1½ to 2 Hrs.	2 Hrs. or More	5
60 to 65 Min.	1 to 1¼ Hrs.	1¼ to 1½ Hrs.	1½ to 2 Hrs.	2 Hrs. or More	5
———	¾ to 1¼ Hrs.	1 to 1½ Hrs.	1¼ to 1¾ Hrs.	2 Hrs. or More	5
———	¾ to 1 Hr.	1 to 1¼ Hrs.	1¼ to 1½ Hrs.	1¾ Hrs. or More	5
	———	———	2 to 2½ Hrs.	2½ to 3½ Hrs.	
———	———	———	———	2 to 4 Hrs.	6
———	———	———	———	2 to 3½ Hrs.	6
———	———	———	———	4 to 6 Hrs.	6
———	———	———	———	1 to 1½ Hrs.	6
———	———	———	———	3 to 4 Hrs.	6
———	———	———	———	1 to 1½ Hrs.	7
———	———	———	———	¾ to 1 Hr.	7
———	———	———	———	¾ to 1 Hr.	7
———	———	———	———	2 to 4 Hrs.	7
———	———	———	———	1¾ to 2½ Hrs.	
———	———	———	———	2 to 3 Hrs.	
		———	———	1 to 1½ Hrs.	8
———	———	———	———	2 to 3 Hrs.	
———	———	———	———	1½ to 2½ Hrs.	
———	———	———	———	¾ to 1½ Hrs.	
1 to 1¼ Hrs.	1¼ to 1½ Hrs.	1½ to 1¾ Hrs.	1¾ to 2¼ Hrs.	2 Hrs. or More	
50 to 65 Min.	1 to 1¼ Hrs.	1¼ to 1½ Hrs.	1½ to 2 Hrs.	2 Hrs. or More	
———	1¼ to 1½ Hrs.	1½ to 1¾ Hrs.	1¾ to 2¼ Hrs.	2 Hrs. or More	

Comments

1. Start with very hot fire; let it burn down to medium.
2. If meat is larded (wrapped in fat), it will take somewhat longer to cook.
3. Handle fire as for rib roast, above.
4. Thawing time varies, depending upon shape of fish.
5. Some believe lamb is tenderer and more flavorsome when cooked rare.
6. Pork should be cooked to 185° internal temperature.
7. Eviscerated weight. Use leg joint test for doneness.
8. Whole wild duck cooks in 20 to 30 minutes to very rare stage.

BEEF

Standing Rib Roast

A rib roast of any size, from 2 ribs to 8, may be roasted to perfection on the spit. Have the ribs cut short and the back cord and chine bone removed. If the roast is larded with fat, it should be securely tied in place. A standing rib roast should be spitted on the diagonal—this makes balancing much easier.

Insert one end of the spit into the cut side just below the ends of the bones. Force it diagonally through the length of the roast, so that it emerges toward the top of the other cut end. Adjust holding forks and tighten screws securely. Balance the roast and respit if necessary. Insert the meat thermometer in the center of the meat, making sure that it will not touch a bone or the spit. Roast over a medium slow fire until the thermometer reaches the point you desire. A 5-rib roast will take from 2 to 2½ hours to reach from 125° to 140°.

Spencer Roast

This is a rib roast with the bone and most of the end fat removed. It may be spitted through the center of the meat, or on a diagonal. It should be securely tied. A whole one, weighing about 14 to 16 pounds, makes a fine roast to serve a large party of 20 or more. It will cook rare in about 2 hours, well done in 3½. Again, we recommend a meat thermometer.

Rolled Rib Roast

This is usually cut from the large end, the bones removed, and the remaining meat and fat tied in a roll. It is most easily spitted if

Rolled beef roast cooks quickly in an electric rotisserie: 1 to 1½ hours for 5 pounds, depending on rareness desired

This broiler barbecues by direct and reflected heat with charcoal held behind meat. Foil-lined pan catches drippings

done on the diagonal. It will take a little longer than a Spencer roast.

It is excellent for serving a crowd; it is easy to slice in convenient serving-size pieces. Have the butcher roll a rib of beef. Make several small incisions in the surface of roast and insert small pieces of peeled onion and fresh thyme. Rub surface of roast lightly with smoked salt. Place on spit and roast, basting frequently with barbecue sauce. Cooking time is 1½ to 2 hours. Slice in rounds to serve. Serves 14.

Tenderloin Roast

Here is a boneless cut that is actually better in a lower grade of beef than prime or choice. Good, standard, or commercial tenderloin makes a fine, tender, and economical roast, as the fat content is less than in the higher grade. It should be basted with butter or oil, or wrapped in fat. Such a roast will cook rare in half an hour. It may be spitted through the center of the meat, but it must be tied securely.

Two mustard-coated legs of lamb cook on revolving spit while foil-wrapped corn roasts and the garlic bread toasts

Boned turkey roll roasts and browns evenly over a low bed of coals. Meat thermometer shows when bird is done

Rump Roast

This is a fine cut for roasting, if "prime" or "choice" beef is used. It should be trimmed and tied compactly. A thermometer is essential with this cut, as the shape varies considerably. For this reason not even approximate timing can be given.

Sirloin Roast

Here is a very choice roast, better known in England than it is here. It is the same cut as a strip or top sirloin or club steak, but it should be cut at least 5 inches thick. Spit on the diagonal, and cook with a thermometer. It will take less than an hour for rare.

VEAL

Veal roasts may be successfully cooked on the spit, but, because of their tendency to be dry, they should be well basted or well larded. Spit in the same manner as like cuts of lamb, and cook until the thermometer reaches 160° to 165°, or until well done.

Calf Liver

A whole calf's liver makes a delectable dish when properly spit roasted. Lard the whole liver (or a 4 or 5-pound piece of beef liver), roll it, and tie it in a compact form. Spit the liver through the middle and roast it to 145° to 150°, if you like liver slightly pink and juicy. Cooking will take about an hour longer if you like liver well done.

LAMB

A leg of lamb or mutton should be spitted more or less parallel to the bone. A rolled boneless shoulder may either be spitted on the diagonal or straight through the meat. Both roasts take about the same length of time to cook: medium rare (145° to 150°) in an hour or a little over, well done up to 2½ hours.

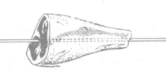

Leg of Lamb

Wipe leg of lamb with a damp cloth. Sprinkle with salt, pepper, and a little flour. Rub into meat. Slash and insert cut pieces of garlic. Place on spit and baste frequently.

Basting sauce:

3 tablespoons Worcestershire	1 tablespoon sugar
3 tablespoons meat sauce	1 tablespoon vinegar
½ cup tomato catsup	2 teaspoons liquid smoke
2 tablespoons butter or margarine	1 medium sized onion, grated
3 tablespoons shortening	1 teaspoon salt
	Few drops Tabasco

Combine ingredients in a small saucepan and heat to boiling.

Saddle and Rack

The saddle and rack of lamb are other good cuts for spit roasting. Have the flank of the saddle rolled inside, and tie compactly. The rack may have the flank folded over the ends of the chops. It, too, should be tied very securely.

Lamb Shoulder

4 cloves garlic, minced	1 pint water
2 large onions, minced	Rosemary and thyme to taste
1 green pepper, minced	
2 tablespoons salt	Dried celery leaves to taste
1 tablespoon freshly ground pepper	Dash of Tabasco
	1 pint red wine
2 cans (6 oz.) tomato paste	4 lamb shoulders

Simmer sauce ingredients except wine for about 1 hour, stirring often. Remove from stove, cool, and stir in the red wine. Place about 1 pint of the sauce in a jar (saving the rest for later, of course) and take it to your favorite butcher. Have the butcher bone the lamb shoulders, cover the insides well with the contents of your jar, and then roll them as any rolled roast.

Bring the rolled roast home, spit it over a good bed of coals, and baste frequently with the remainder of the sauce. Cooking time 1½ to 2 hours. Serves 24 (6 to each lamb shoulder).

Breast

Breast of lamb makes a good inexpensive meat for charcoal roasting. Have it left whole and weave it on the spit, in the manner of spareribs. It is best when basted with a rather highly seasoned sauce or marinade.

Kidneys

Lamb kidneys are delicious when cooked on the spit. Have them left in their fat, and tie more pounded fat over them where they are exposed. Impale 6 or 8 of them on the spit and fasten holding forks at both ends. Run an extra long skewer through all of them diagonally. Roast for 25 to 45 minutes, depending on the degree of doneness you prefer.

PORK

A fresh shoulder or ham may be nicely roasted over charcoal. It should be done slowly and cooked to 175°. It will then be safely cooked but not dried out. A 12-pound fresh ham takes 4 hours or more. Spit like lamb.

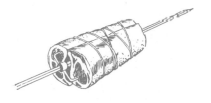

Pork loins make a fine roast. Two loins may be tied together so that the fat is on the outside giving the appearance of a rolled piece of meat. Spit through the center. A single loin takes from 2 to 2½ hours to cook.

Suckling pigs are spectacular and delicious. Select one weighing 18 pounds or less. Tie the legs together and truss them close to the body. The pig may be stuffed, if desired. Cook, brushing with heavy cream or butter occasionally, for 3 to 4 hours, or until the thermometer reaches a temperature of 185°. (See page 88.)

Spit roasting is an ideal way to cook spareribs, as they will cook slowly without flaring. They should be left in one piece and woven on the spit. Basting is usually preferred. The ribs will cook to a shiny tender brown in from 1 to 1½ hours. Do not overcook or the meat will be dry.

Barbecued Ham

Make your fire of prune or fruit wood, approximately two or three inches in diameter, and enough charcoal to keep the bed of coals at an even heat. Lay a 7-pound shank of tenderized ham directly on the grill for about 15 minutes on each side. Then take it off the fire and remove the skin. Leave fat on and score.

Spit, or skewer, the ham and cook it from 3½ to 4 hours, basting it as it cooks. The outside fat will char black, but don't let that worry you. Just don't let it burn. Keep the fire constant.

When ham is done, break off charred fat with a knife. Put back on spit for another 10 or 15 minutes and use up remainder of basting sauce. Remove ham, cut off excess fat, slice, and serve. Serves 6 to 8.

Basting sauce:

1 tablespoon cinnamon	2 tablespoons brown sugar
1 tablespoon dry mustard	1/2 tablespoon molasses
1 tablespoon ginger	2/3 cup wine vinegar
1/2 tablespoon whole cloves	Pineapple juice
1 1/2 to 2 ounces whiskey or gin	

Place the cinnamon, mustard, ginger, and cloves in a mortar, or small jar, and cover with the whiskey or gin. (The alcohol will dissolve the essential oils, and that's what gives the flavor.) Let set for an hour or so. Put the brown sugar, molasses, and vinegar in a pint jar. Grind the spices with a pestle, or stir well, and add to the vinegar-sugar solution. Pour in enough pineapple juice to make a pint. Stir well.

Now you are ready to paint your ham. Mix the sauce each time you baste, so that the spices are evenly distributed. Don't leave any dregs in the jar, put them all on the ham to get the full, spicy flavor.

Roast Suckling Pig

Ask your butcher to provide you with a cleaned, tender suckling pig about 15-20 pounds in weight. A young pig any smaller will be nothing but skin and bones when cooked.

Stuff with a sage or fruit dressing. Don't stuff it in too tightly, as the dressing will expand. Sew it in with heavy string and lace it closely and tightly.

Leave the skin on. Head and feet can be cut off either before or after cooking; it is easier done before—but it won't look much like a pig. Insert a piece of wood in the mouth to simplify adding an apple later. Truss the legs with cord in a kneeling position, and place pig on spit over a deep bed of hot coals. Coals should be arranged in such a way to allow for a pan to be placed in the center to catch the drippings from the roasting meat; drippings should be used for basting. The pig can be basted with oil, but it will lose some of its flavor. Cooking time: 6 to 10 hours, depending on the fire.

When done, remove from the spit, place a red apple in the mouth, cranberries or cherries in the eye sockets, and place it on a bed of watercress. Various garnishes of vegetable flowers, radish roses, stuffed stewed apricots and prunes, or holly berries, may be added.

Bring the roast pig to the table with the head separated from the body, the cut ringed with a wreath of watercress and flowers. In carving, first separate the shoulder from the carcass, and remove the legs. This will leave the ribs open to the knife. Cut down the backbone, remove the loins and serve the tender chops from sliced loins.

Leg of Pork

A leg of pork may be barbecued on the spit (or grill)—providing you keep a bed of coals going for 8 to 9 hours.

Place a 14 to 16-pound leg on the spit, shield it if possible to keep in all the heat, and roast for 6 or 7 hours before basting. Cook for about 2 hours longer, basting frequently with Southern Barbecue Sauce, recipe on page 122.

Garlic Spareribs

6 pounds (or more) spareribs	1 cup orange marmalade
4 large cloves garlic	1/4 cup vinegar
1 tablespoon salt	1/4 cup catsup
1 cup chicken stock or consommé	

Figure on at least 1 pound of spareribs per person. Leave the sides whole so you can thread them on a spit later. Crush the garlic with the salt. Add the chicken stock, marmalade, vinegar, and catsup. Marinate the spareribs for at least 12 hours in the garlic marinade, turning several times. Weave the whole strips on a spit, and cook over low coals for 1 to 1½ hours, or until shiny brown and fork tender. Baste with the marinade during the cooking. Serves 6.

Barbecued Bologna Roll

Remove casing from large round bologna. Score top surface as you do for ham. Insert spit down center. Grill over coals, basting frequently with barbecue sauce.

FOWL

Roast Chicken Parts

Thaw frozen drumsticks, breasts, and thighs from 8 packages, and soak for 2 hours in the following marinade:

1½ cups soy	1 finger fresh ginger root, shredded
½ cup water	
¼ cup salad oil	2 cloves garlic, minced
¼ cup gin	1/3 cup sugar

Put marinated chicken in wire basket and fasten it to spit to revolve over large but low fire (no hood). Baste with remaining marinade until chicken is done. (This will take an hour or more.) Recipe serves 10 to 12 people.

Chicken

This makes a fine spit-roasted meal. Truss it compactly and spit from just in front of the tail (through the bone), diagonally to a point near the apex of the wishbone (again through the bone, which is very soft at this point). A chicken is best basted occasionally. It may or may not be stuffed. It will cook in 1 to 1½ hours, depending on its size and tenderness. The best test for doneness is to wiggle the leg—when it moves easily at the joint, the chicken is done.

Turkey

It may be stuffed or not. It will probably take a little longer stuffed, as the heat penetrates slowly. Spit in the same way as chicken; you may need a hammer to drive the spit through the breastbone. A 15-pound turkey—dressed weight—will take about 3 hours to roast. Test it by moving the leg, or insert a thermometer in the fleshy part of the thigh and cook to 170° to 175°. (Remember that all large roasts continue cooking after they are removed from the heat of the fire.)

Chicken parts are strung on spit. Corn catches dripping juices from meat. Saute mixed fruits on top in butter

Roast Turkey

Remove bird from refrigerator 2 or 3 hours before cooking. Loosen neck skin and cut off neck close to the body, leaving the flap of skin. Put neck, heart, and gizzard to cook in about 1½ quarts of water with several sprigs of parsley and celery tops, and a sliced onion; simmer until very tender, then drop in the liver and cook 15 minutes longer. Set aside to use in making stuffing and/or gravy. Rub inside of bird with salt and pepper, then stuff with dressing.

Stitch or skewer the flap of neck skin to back of bird, and sew up or skewer and lace the body opening. Truss bird into compact shape, and slide on spit. Test it for balance, then lock in place with locking tines. Rub it all over with melted turkey fat or oil, and place bird in position over coals. As it cooks, baste with Chicken or Turkey Sauce, page 125.

Clear an oval in the coals and place a pan in center of the ring of coals to catch drippings from the roasting bird. Scoop out drippings with a long-handled spoon and add to basting sauce.

Bread stuffing:

Allow about 1 cup bread crumbs for each pound dressed weight.

3 quarts soft white bread crumbs	2 medium sized onions chopped
1 to 2 teaspoons rubbed sage, thyme, or marjoram (or all three)	1 cup celery tops, finely chopped
2 to 3 teaspoons salt	¾ to 1 cup melted butter or margarine
½ teaspoon black pepper	1 cup broth from cooked giblets

Duck, Goose

Duck, goose, and other birds are trussed and spitted in the same manner as chickens. A duck will take 1¼ to 1¾ hours; a junior goose, from 1¾ to 2½ hours; a regular goose, 2 to 3 hours. A squab takes about ¾ of an hour or more; a Cornish game hen will cook in less than an hour; and wild ducks and wild geese will cook in 15 minutes to 45 minutes (for duck), and 45 minutes to 1½ hours (for geese), depending upon how rare you like them.

Roast Duck Colby

2 frozen ducks, 4½ pounds each	½ teaspoon thyme
6 large or 10 small day-old French rolls	¼ teaspoon garlic powder
	¼ teaspoon onion powder
1 can (10 oz.) Pacific oysters (8 to a can)	8 stalks celery, strings removed, and very thinly sliced
1 can mixed nuts, coarsely chopped	¼ teaspoon black pepper

Let the ducks thaw; then dry them thoroughly inside and out.

To prepare stuffing, cut rolls into cubes and pour liquid from oysters over them. Cut oysters into small pieces and add them and also all the remaining ingredients, working all together with the hands. Stuff the ducks with this mixture, sew them up, and place them on a revolving spit. Cook for 4½ hours. (NOTE: *The time, naturally, may vary with the heat of the coals.*)

Just before serving the ducks, make brown gravy from the pan drippings and add the sliced cooked giblets. Serve Burgundy wine with the dinner. Serves 8.

Roast Goose

Buy a small (6 to 9-pound) goose. If the goose has been frozen, be sure it is completely thawed, and dried thoroughly. Rub the inside with salt and a cut half of lemon.

Spit the goose, securing it firmly. Roast over medium coals for 1¾ to 2½ hours, or until it is fork tender and the skin is crisp. (We have found that 2¼ hours is long enough for a 6 to 7-pound goose.)

FISH/SEAFOOD

Because fish tends to fall apart when cooked, it is usually more satisfactory to broil split fish or fish steaks, or even a whole fish. However, if the whole fish is wrapped well in chicken wire and fastened securely, it may be spit roasted. Insert the spit the length of the fish, in the center, and use holding forks.

The best fish for roasting whole are salmon, sturgeon, bass, tuna, or any large firm fleshed fish. Roasting will take from 30 to 60 minutes, depending on size. A fish is done when the thermometer reaches 155° or 160°, or when the flesh flakes easily with a fork. Be careful not to overcook any fish.

Smaller fish may be spit roasted, but it is questionable whether this isn't more trouble than it's worth. The fish broils so quickly that the extra time spent in spitting is probably wasted. However, if it is done, put several fish on one spit, spitting them through the middle, sideways, have one head faced one way, the next in the opposite direction, alternating the length of the spit.

To spit roast whole albacore, remove head, tail, side fins. Brush cavity with marinade, close up, skewer, tie at 1-inch intervals. Center on spit and barbecue for 1 hour, basting often with marinade

Slicing rolled tuna is a little difficult because of fish's triangular bone structure. First cut down to the bones with sharp, thin-bladed knife. Saw through the bones with a heavy, serrated knife

Lobster

Whole lobsters may be spitted right through their shells, from head to tail. They will cook to a juicy tenderness in 12 to 15 minutes.

Charcoal-Roasted Liver

Select a whole calf or lamb liver, and tie it into a compact piece. Lard it or tie strips of salt pork on the outside. Fasten on the spit and rotate over a medium hot fire for about an hour, or until a meat thermometer reads 150° for juicily pink, 160° for well done. Serve this delicious meat, sliced fairly thin, with new potatoes in parsley butter, and onions wrapped in foil and roasted in the coals. Roasted corn is good with it, too.

Charcoal-Broiled Tongue

Tongue needs pre-cooking, but it's very good broiled until crusty outside. Cook tongue in a pressure cooker or in boiling water until tender. Drain, skin, and trim. Put tongue on spit and cook over charcoal for about 45 minutes, basting with ½ cup melted butter, ½ cup dry white table wine, and 1 teaspoon *each* chopped chives, parsley, and tarragon.

Spit-Roasted Fruits or Vegetables

If your barbecue equipment has multiple spits, you may like to spit-roast some fruits and vegetables. They will take longer to cook by this method than by ash-roasting, but they will be more uniformly cooked. Whole green peppers, acorn squash, potatoes, onions, yams, apples, and eggplant can all be cooked in this manner.

Skewer cooking

When you decide to have a skewer dinner, toss rules and cookbooks aside. Just take an assortment of foods from refrigerator and cupboard, season them with imagination and curiosity, push on a skewer, add a bit of showmanship, and grill over coals. Anything and everything which cooks in a reasonable length of time can go on a long or short metal skewer.

All kinds of meat, firm fish and shellfish, canned meats and sausages, almost any vegetable, and many fruits can be slipped over steel spikes for their turn over the grill. Pre-cooking gives you an even greater choice. Best of all, you have both meat and vegetables on one skewer, needing only some rice, a glistening green salad, and a well-browned loaf of French bread treated with garlic butter to complete the meal.

An assortment of food grilled on a skewer is colorful and gay. There's no monotony with such a meal because each bite is different—something like a box of assorted chocolates. And, if the foods have hugged close together while they cooked, they'll slide off the skewer and retain their shape on the plate.

Preparing vegetables: Cut small onions lengthwise twice to quarter them. Do the same with unpeeled tomatoes; cut out stem ends. Split green peppers, remove seeds, stems, and cut into eighths. Pull the stems from mushroom caps

1

To ruffle round steak strips, start with trimmed piece of meat 1 to 1½ inches thick. Cut into thin slices across the grain of meat to shorten long fibers, tenderize meat. Thread several strips onto skewer, dip them in soy, then grill

2

Even the shape that the food takes on a skewer can be varied. Instead of using green pepper squares, curve green pepper strips around another bite of food. In addition to looking attractive, the green pepper will keep fragile foods such as fruit from breaking off the skewer. Instead of cutting bacon or beef into squares, try weaving strips of either meat on the skewer. The trick to this is to use the skewer as you would a long needle and a short piece of thread and work close to the point.

Onions cut into quarters stay put if the skewer is run through the point and out on the other side. Tomato quarters will still be intact if they aren't too ripe and if the skin is left on to hold them together. Since mushrooms may split and fall into the coals if pressed too hard in the line-up, they are better when they are used as end pieces.

Bacon squares or strips and partially cooked sausage add fat and flavor to lean foods such as vegetables and fish or shellfish. Use oil, butter, or margarine in the basting sauce, too, to help with the browning as well as to add fat to some foods. Any barbecue sauce should be heated so that it won't cool off the foods on the grill and will have a better chance to season well.

3

4

Green peppers for shish kebab are less likely to split and fall off the skewer during cooking if you take a knife and cut out a small crater at each end to act as a "pilot hole" for the skewer. This is true for other crisp vegetables

Grill loaded skewers over low coals, basting often with a marinade to suit the food. Pictured here are just two of the many combinations you can prepare for skewer cooking: Raw prawns and pork sausage, left; shish kebab, right

It's up to the cook to decide whether or not to soak the filled skewers in a marinade before grilling—except in the case of shish kebab. Here the squares of meat cut from a leg of lamb must be marinated (preferably overnight) so that the herb and garlic-flavored wine and oil goes clear through them. Round steak strips or squares are better flavored and take on a crisper brown if soaked in a mixture of soy sauce and a little mashed garlic. Worcestershire sauce performs in much the same way.

For a new idea in patio entertaining, you can give your guests a chance to build their own dinners on skewers. Spread out an assortment of foods on a tray, furnish skewers and paper napkins, and see who will come up with the most amazing assortment—the "Dagwoods" of the grill. But it isn't wise to let each guest cook his own skewer meal after assembling it. That would be asking for burned meat and trouble. Here, however, is where the host can perform with mop and sauces.

Try a Skewer Buffet

Everybody has fun at a skewer buffet—the guest because he can select his own combination of food to slip on the steel spike;

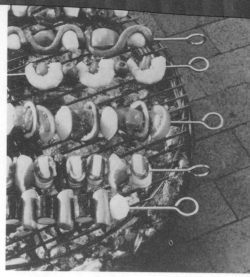

Fireplace shish kebab rack is driven by a spit motor. The rack, which revolves slowly, holds six full skewers. The small, four-pronged wheel at left end of each skewer hits a stop once each revolution, moving skewer 1/4 turn

A more common method of barbecuing skewered foods is over the coals of an outdoor grill. Here you see the variety of ingredients that can be cooked in same fashion. See following pages for a variety of skewer combination ideas

Mutton cubes are skewered on this multiple spit which is chain driven by the electric motor in the foreground.

Five rows of coals are placed so that each is directly under a skewer with aluminum "drip pans" between rows

the host because he holds the center of the stage at the barbecue, basting and browning each personalized order; and the hostess because most of her work is done before the party starts.

A good assortment of skewer foods is colorful and gay looking. Best of all, foods can be simple. You can plan your buffet around several kinds of meat or fish. Add half a dozen vegetables, and fruits—and endless combinations are possible.

You can thread on a skewer any food that cooks in a reasonable length of time. Remember, however, that you can't mix short-cooking and long-cooking foods on the same steel spike.

To baste as large an assortment of foods as is shown on pages 100-101, you will need three different sauces:

Sauce No. 1: Soy, wine, and oil seasoned with mashed garlic.

Sauce No. 2: Tomato-base barbecue sauce.

Sauce No. 3: Lemon-butter seasoned with herbs.

You may wish to marinate some of the meats before arranging them in dishes. In this case, save the marinade, add extra oil

Turkey teriyaki can be prepared by broiling skewered slices of turkey meat that have marinated in a mixture of 1 cup sherry, 4 cloves garlic, 1 crushed ginger root, and ¼ cup of soy for 1 hour. Broil over hot coals in hibachi

or butter to insure better browning, and heat the mixture over the grill before using it as a basting sauce.

Here are the nine skewer combinations shown in the photograph above:

1. **Round steak with small green onion bulbs.** Weave strips of meat around onion bulbs on skewer, working close to the point of skewer. Grill. (Sauce No. 1.)

2. **Bacon-pineapple roll-ups; sweet pickle chunks.** Grill slowly until bacon is done. Drippings provide natural basting sauce. Bacon keeps pineapple from falling off skewer.

3. **Green pepper strips; whole small, white boiling onions (or canned onions); bacon; round steak strips.** Roll up thin round steak strips loosely so meat cooks in center. Bacon supplies some fat. Grill slowly. (Sauce No. 1 or No. 2.)

onion bulbs; chicken livers; canned artichoke hearts; unpeeled tomato sections; mushroom caps; green peppers, pimientos; stuffed green olive-ham roll-ups, steak strips, bacon; orange wedges, apple slices; lamb squares; bacon-pineapple roll-ups; cooked, shucked prawns; ham squares, frankfurters in sections

4. **Orange sections; ham and olive roll-ups.** Ham supplies some fat so light basting of oil is sufficient.

5. **Onion quarters; marinated lamb; green pepper; tomato.** Add additional oil or butter to marinade for sauce.

6. **Apple and ham.** Butter or oil provides necessary fat; last-minute brushing with honey glazes meat, fruit.

7. **Mushrooms; bacon; chicken livers.** Weave bacon around chicken livers. Grill slowly. (Sauce No. 1 or No. 3.)

8. **Ripe olives; prawns; pimiento.** Food is cooked so needs only browning. (Sauce No. 3.)

9. **Potato; chunks of frankfurter; canned artichoke hearts.** Use cooked small potatoes or canned potatoes. Skewer artichokes through the hearts. Needs only heating, browning. (Sauce No. 3 plus some prepared mustard.)

LAMB

Lamb en Brochette

4 tablespoons olive oil	1 large onion, grated fine
6 tablespoons soy sauce	3 tablespoons lemon juice
1/4 teaspoon freshly ground pepper	3 to 4 pounds lean lamb meat

Mix ingredients together to make a marinade. Cut lamb into cubes and leave in the marinade for an hour or longer, turning and rubbing the seasonings into the meat. Thread on skewers and broil. Serves 6.

Marinated Lamb

5 pound leg of lamb	1/2 cup sherry
1/2 pound onions, peeled, sliced	2 tablespoons olive oil
1 tablespoon salt	1 teaspoon oregano
1/2 teaspoon pepper	

Night before the barbecue, trim fat and gristle from the leg of lamb and cut lean meat into 2-inch cubes. Put in a large bowl and mix with a sauce made of the ingredients above. Leave in marinade overnight. Put 4 to 6 cubes of meat on skewers and grill for 15 to 20 minutes or longer. Serves 4.

Shish Kebab

Buy 1 pound of leg of lamb per person, plus 2 or 3 extra pounds. Lamb shoulder may be used, too. Plan on 1 1/3 "shish" (skewer load) per person.

1 medium sized onion per person	1/2 cup wine, wine vinegar, or cider vinegar
Salt	2 tablespoons olive oil
Cayenne	1 medium sized green pepper per "shish"
Italian red pepper	1 1/2 medium sized tomatoes per "shish"
Black pepper	
1 package or jar dried oregano (you won't use all of it)	

A day ahead of time prepare the meat as follows: Cut the boned leg of lamb into steaks, crosswise down the length of the leg, about 1¼ inches to 1½ inches thick; then into cubes. Cut out any gristle. A small strip of fat may be left on the cubes if desired.

Place meat in a bowl and salt to taste. Pepper with the three different kinds of pepper, but not too much for it will kill the flavor of the meat. Add about 1 rounded tablespoon of oregano for each leg of lamb. Cut onions into thin strips and place in the bowl with the meat. Pour over all the wine or vinegar and olive oil. Mix well and allow this to marinate in your refrigerator overnight.

Save the lamb bones and leftovers to make the broth used in preparing pilaff, an accompanying rice dish, the recipe for which is given in the chapter on accompaniments.

Cut the tomatoes into chunks about the same size as the meat. Do not skin. Small Italian pear-shaped tomatoes are good used whole. Cut the peppers into pieces big enough to bend and be skewered. Beginning with a piece of meat, then tomato, and pepper, skewer three of each alternately on each "shish." Broil for 15 to 20 minutes over a good bed of coals, basting frequently.

Heat the marinade, add chopped tomatoes to suit taste, and use for sauce.

Lamb in Onion Juice

2 pounds lean lamb	½ teaspoon thyme
2 medium sized onions	Pinch of sage
½ cup salad oil	3 peppercorns, crushed
1 bay leaf	1 cup sherry (or red wine)
1 teaspoon salt	

Cut the lamb into cubes about an inch square and put them in an earthen bowl. Run the two onions through the food grinder, using the finest blade. Place the onion pulp in a small muslin sack or a cloth and squeeze the juice onto the meat. Add the oil, bay leaf, and seasonings, working them into the meat. Add the wine and let everything stand—at least overnight. Then spike the meat on skewers and broil to your taste. You can alternate pieces of bacon, onion, green peppers, or even very small tomatoes with the lamb.

Lamb Combinations

String skewers with lamb cubes, alternating with small, ripe, unpeeled tomatoes and small peeled onions; or squares of bacon and mushrooms; or cubes of parboiled eggplant (brushed with oil) and wedges of tomatoes.

Lamb and Ham Shish Kebab

Using about 7 pounds of shoulder or leg of lamb for 7-8 people, cut the lamb in cubes.

Soak 6-8 hours in claret wine—enough to almost cover meat; add slices of onion and garlic to your taste.

Place on skewers, alternating the lamb with small pieces of tenderized ham. Season with salt and pepper. Broil over charcoal fire.

Skewered Minted Lamb

For each serving, use:

3 pieces lean lamb, cut in squares
2 whole small green tomatoes

2 slices onion, cut 1/2 inch thick
6 squares sliced bacon

Marinate meat for 30 minutes in sauce given below. Alternate the above items on skewers. Broil, basting frequently with sauce until done. Serve with rice, sour French bread, and tossed green salad.

Marinade and basting sauce:

1/2 ounce dry mint leaves
1 teaspoon dry tarragon leaves
1/2 cup vinegar
3/4 cup brown sugar
1 teaspoon dry mustard

1/2 teaspoon salt
1/2 cup butter
Juice of 1/2 lemon and grated peel
1/2 cup sauterne

Put all ingredients except sauterne into a saucepan and bring to a boil. Remove from heat, cover pan, and let steep for about 30 minutes. Strain, and add sauterne. Cool.

Chinese Shish Kebab

Dip cubes of lamb or pork in a mixture of soy sauce, cornstarch, and peanut oil. If available, add fresh ginger root, mashed. Skewer between slices of green pepper and cook over coals. Serve with sauce made from 1 part prepared mustard to 3 parts catsup.

Lamb or Beef Kebabs

1½ pounds meat (use either beef round or lamb shoulder) cut in 1-inch cubes	2 tablespoons beefsteak sauce
½ cup tomato catsup	2 tablespoons cider vinegar
1 teaspoon salt	2 tablespoons Worcestershire
2 tablespoons sugar	¼ cup water
	2 tablespoons salad oil or shortening

Place cubed meat in bowl; combine remaining ingredients in saucepan and heat to boiling. Pour over meat; let stand several hours or overnight in marinade. String on skewers and broil over hot coals. Reheat marinating liquid for sauce. Serves 4.

Lamb Liver

1 whole lamb liver (1-1½ pounds)	4 cloves garlic, mashed Salt and allspice to taste
5 medium sized onions	1 large bunch celery

Buy the freshest lamb liver you can get. Cut it into 1-inch cubes and place in bowl. Add onions, cut in 4 parts lengthwise (do not cut the bottom stem, just peel outside skin, otherwise the onion sections will fall apart). Add the mashed garlic and seasonings. Chop the bunch of celery, including the leaves, and place in bowl. Mix all ingredients together and set in refrigerator for 2 hours.

Place on skewers, alternating an onion quarter with 3 or 4 cubes of liver, and broil. Use remaining vegetables for salad. Serves 2 to 4.

Foil Kebabs

To cook kebabs in foil: Thread meat, onion, green pepper, and tomato cubes on a skewer or a thin stick. Wrap in a double thickness of foil, place on coals, and cook for about 14 minutes.

BEEF

Rolled Steak

Slice sirloin tip across the grain with a very sharp knife, making thin slices about the size of the palm of the hand. Cut fat bacon lengthwise into narrow strips about ⅛-inch wide. Put a strip inside the slice of beef and roll up; pin with toothpicks. Slide roll on skewer and broil.

Beef Skirts-Kebabs

On a beef, there is a strip running along the bottom of each flank called a skirt steak. Two of these adequately serve four persons. Get your butcher to cut these skirts in two, lengthwise, and you will wind up with four long pieces of meat about 2 inches wide and 18 inches long.

2 skirt steaks, cut into 4 lengthwise strips	2 tablespoons soy sauce
¼ cup salad or olive oil	2 tablespoons prepared mustard
1 cup dry red wine	Fresh mushroom caps, quartered; onions, green peppers, and tomatoes as desired
1 clove garlic, crushed	
1 medium sized onion, minced or grated	
½ teaspoon pepper	

Soak the meat in the marinade (all the remaining ingredients except the mushrooms, onions, peppers, tomatoes) for at least 5 hours—the longer the better.

When the charcoal fire is ready, thread the meat on metal skewers in a ribbon style, alternating with mushrooms and other whole ingredients.

The fire should be 6 to 8 inches from the skewers. Cooking time is between 45 minutes and 1 hour. When you serve, give each of your guests a Skirt-Kebab, sliding it deftly off the skewer. This is a wonderful accompaniment to lasagna, a green salad, and garlic French bread. Serves 4.

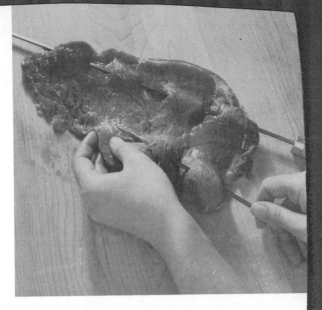

RIPPLE SKEWERING. *Work close to skewer's point as you weave it in meat. Leave 1½ inches between each "stitch"*

Skewered Round Steak

Buy whole slices of top round, cut ⅜ inch thick. Allow 1 slice for 3 people (or for 2 if they have "outdoor" appetites). Weave meat on 2 skewers so the length of the meat runs parallel to the skewers. Weave skewers about 1 to 1½ inches in from the side edges of the meat. Rub both sides of meat with a cut clove of garlic and salad oil.

Hold meat over low coals 3 minutes for each side, or until half done. Sprinkle with salt, pepper, and any other seasonings you wish; then using 2 forks, bunch the meat together on the skewers so it "ripples." Continue cooking until each side is crusty brown.

Pull meat off skewers and cut crosswise in 2 or 3 servings. The sections of meat folded inside the ripples will be rare and juicy and the outside sections will be crusty. For an even better browning, brush the meat with a barbecue sauce after you have bunched it together in ripples.

Beef Combinations

String skewers with cubes of beef with dividers of: onion quarters and tomato wedges; squares of pre-cooked pork, dipped in beaten egg and crumbs and brushed with oil or shortening; or squares of ham and pineapple wedges.

Skewered Steak and Mushrooms

Well marinated squares of tender beef, and fresh mushrooms, threaded on skewers and broiled, make good outdoor eating.

1/2 cup Burgundy or claret wine	1/2 teaspoon monosodium
1 teaspoon Worcestershire	glutamate
1 clove garlic	1 tablespoon vinegar
1/2 cup salad oil	1/2 teaspoon marjoram
2 tablespoons catsup	1/2 teaspoon rosemary
1 teaspoon sugar	1 pound sirloin steak
1/2 teaspoon salt	12 large fresh mushrooms

Mix wine with Worcestershire, peeled garlic clove, salad oil, catsup, and seasonings. Cut meat into 2-inch squares. Wash mushrooms thoroughly. Marinate steak squares and mushrooms in wine mixture for 2 hours.

Alternate meat squares and mushrooms on skewers. Broil, turning on all sides, basting frequently with remaining marinade. Serves 4.

Steak Kebabs

Secure bay tree sticks from the hills. (Any green sticks may be used but the bay sticks add aroma and flavor.) Wash and whittle them to a point at the smaller end.

Pieces of steak cut about 3 or 4 inches square are spiked on the stick, leaving about an inch or so between each 2 pieces. This, of course, is to allow the meat to cook on all sides. Salt and pepper the meat and then hold or prop your stick over the fire until the meat is done to your own liking. It usually takes 20 to 30 minutes. Top round steak from good beef may be used for this.

Liver

Skewer calves-liver cubes with bacon and whole mushrooms. For chicken livers, alternate with small bacon squares. Broil.

When you skewer, leave 1-inch space
between chunks so meat cooks evenly
When the chunks are cooked, take the
loaded skewer to cutting board. Place
the point of skewer down on the board
and slide the chunks down, very close
together. With sharp knife, cut down
through the chunks across the grain

Skewered Beef Chunks

Fillet of beef or top round, cut 3 inches thick.

Sauce:

1/2 cup olive oil	1 tablespoon paprika
3 tablespoons wine vinegar	1 teaspoon monosodium
1/2 tablespoon garlic salt	glutamate

Trim fat, then cut meat in 3-inch squares. Thread 3 cubes on each
skewer, so the grain of the meat is at right angles to the skewer.
Leave 1 inch between each chunk of meat. (If you use lightweight
skewers that are not grooved or notched, stick 2 skewers into each
set of chunks so the meat won't slide around.)

Brush meat with sauce and let stand for 30 minutes. Brush
sauce over meat again, then barbecue until meat is cooked, about
20 to 30 minutes.

To slice meat, place point of skewer on cutting board; slide
chunks down, very close together. Cut down through chunks,
across the grain, and make thin slices. Serve slices on hot split
and buttered French rolls. Have mustard and catsup ready in case
they are desired.

Ground Beef

1 pound ground meat	1 tablespoon prepared
2 eggs	mustard
1/2 cup dry bread crumbs	1/2 teaspoon salt

Combine ground meat with eggs (beaten), bread crumbs, mustard, and salt. Divide into 6 or 8 parts and squeeze each portion of meat around the skewer. Broil. Serves 6 to 8.

Variation:

Use the above combination of ground beef and form into 6 or 8 thick patties; encircle each with a strip of bacon and let stand for several hours. Skewer patties crosswise.

Skewered Hamburger

Garlic, finely chopped	1 pound ground beef
Salt and pepper	1/2 cup finely chopped onion
1/2 cup olive oil	

Put finely chopped garlic, salt, and pepper into olive oil and stir thoroughly. Place hamburger in large bowl and cover with onion. Add olive oil mixture, and combine. Knead with hands to mix onions thoroughly through meat and to permit complete absorption of oil.

Take barbecue skewers and form meat around skewers to about 1½-inch diameter. Length of meat along skewer may be varied to suit size of buns into which it will be placed. Barbecue over charcoal, turning continuously to keep juices in and upon meat.

Push meat off skewers into buns and serve. Have mustard and catsup ready in case it's needed. Serves 6.

Hamburgers en Brochette

Form seasoned meat loaf mixture into balls the size of a small egg. String 2 or 3 meat balls on skewers, alternating with onion and quarters of unpeeled tomato. Sprinkle with salt or brush with barbecue sauce. Grill until done.

Variation:

Mold seasoned meat around skewer, and wrap with a slice of bacon. Dip in sauce when done.

Veal Sati

2 pounds veal steak, cut in
    1-inch squares

1/4 cup soy sauce
Juice of 1 lemon
2 tablespoons oil

Run each skewer through the center of 4 to 6 meat squares. Mix the rest of the ingredients and pour over the skewered meat. Let stand 3 or 4 hours. Broil over glowing coals 15 to 20 minutes, or till a golden brown. Turn as necessary to cook evenly and baste with the sauce once during the broiling. Serves 4 to 6.

Skewered Veal Barbecue

1/3 cup soy sauce
1 large onion, chopped
2 tablespoons salad or olive oil
1 tablespoon dried oregano

2 or 3 veal steaks, 1/2 to 3/4 inch
    thick
Burgundy or claret wine
1 can (No. 2 1/2) sliced pine-
    apple

Mix together the soy, onion, oil, and oregano. Cut the veal steaks into 1 to 1½-inch squares, depending on the thickness of your skewers. Put the veal squares in a bowl, pour in the marinade, then add enough Burgundy to cover the meat when packed down in the bowl. Let the meat marinate all day and turn it in the marinade from time to time. Cut the pineapple slices into quarters.

About 2 hours before time to barbecue, string the meat on the skewers with a piece of pineapple between every two pieces of meat. You'll have to work carefully on the pineapple as it is apt to split if skewers are large. Arrange the skewers on a shallow pan, pour over the sauce and marinate, turning occasionally, until time to barbecue over coals. Barbecuing takes about 20 minutes in all, turning 4 times. Baste with the marinade when you turn skewers. This fills 6 good-sized skewers. If you have any pine-apple left over, drain well, then sauté the pieces in small amount of butter until lightly browned.

Parboiled Sausage

Parboil sausage briefly and string with slices or cubes of unpeeled apple.

FOWL

Skewered Chicken Livers

18 chicken livers
6 slices bacon
  Salt and pepper
  Mushrooms
  Olive oil

Bread crumbs
Butter, melted
Lemon juice
Parsley

Cut away gall from chicken livers, and dry well with clean cloth. Season with pinch of salt and pepper. Cut livers in half. Broil bacon slices, one minute to each side, and cut each slice into 6 pieces.

Take 6 skewers, run one through center of liver slice, then a mushroom, then a piece of bacon, and repeat until all skewers are filled. Roll in olive oil, dip in fresh bread crumbs, and broil over coals.

Arrange on a hot dish, and over them pour melted butter to which lemon juice and chopped parsley have been added. Serves 6.

Chicken Livers With Water Chestnuts

Use fresh (wash thoroughly) or canned water chestnuts; slice into 3 parts. Slice chicken livers and dip in soy sauce; place slice of water chestnut between two slices of chicken liver, wrap in thin strip of bacon, place on skewer, and broil.

Broiled Chicken Hearts

Many "chicken parts" markets sell hearts at a very low price. They are delicious when broiled, either as a main course with a casserole of rice or noodles, or as an appetizer. Marinate washed hearts in equal parts soy, sherry, and cooking oil, seasoning with garlic or ginger, if you wish. String on skewers and broil for about 8 or 9 minutes, turning to cook on both sides.

Campfire Oysters

Use skewers, or cut long green sticks, peel and sharpen ends. Cut thin strips of bacon into fourths. Alternate on the stick with drained oysters, ending and beginning with a piece of bacon. Three large oysters and four pieces of bacon are sufficient for one sandwich. Cook until bacon is well broiled and edges of oysters curl. Push off onto bread or bun. Season with salt and pepper and squeeze a little lemon juice over oysters.

Fish

Cut marinated fish fillets into small cubes or slices, skewer with a wedge of tomato and a tiny piece of bayleaf between each portion.

Shrimp

Skewer whole large shrimps or prawns with dividers of pineapple wedges and bacon. Broil.

Variation:

Peel large shrimps. Dip in soy sauce, drain, skewer, and broil over coals.

FRUITS/ VEGETABLES

This method of cookery requires a slow fire and careful watching. Most fruits cook quickly, but the vegetables, in many cases, should be parboiled first. The pieces are strung on skewers and are usually basted during the broiling.

Fruits

Unpeeled apple quarters. Roll in melted butter and sprinkle with sugar.

Peeled Apple. Cut in cubes, wrap in bacon, and broil until the bacon is crisp.

Peeled Apple. Cut in cubes, wrap in bacon, and broil until the bacon is crisp.

Canned Apricot Halves. Dip in butter after skewering, and broil until brown.

Peeled Bananas. (1) Cut in 4 pieces, dip in melted butter, and brown. Then roll in chopped salted almonds. (2) Cut in 1-inch slices, wrap in bacon, and broil until bacon is crisp.

Orange or Tangerine sections. Dip in butter and broil lightly.

Pineapple Chunks. (1) Alternate with green pepper squares and brush with butter. Cook until lightly browned, but with the pepper still crisp. (2) Alternate with bacon squares; cook until bacon is crisp. (3) Brush with butter; alternate with thin slices of preserved ginger.

Vegetables

Unpeeled Eggplant Cubes. Marinate in garlic-flavored olive oil, and alternate with cherry tomatoes on the skewers. Cook until the eggplant is brown and tender.

Peeled Eggplant Cubes. (1) Wrap in bacon; broil until bacon is crisp. (2) Marinate in French dressing; alternate with green pepper and 1-inch-long pieces of green onion. Broil tender.

Mushroom Caps. (1) Dip in dill-seasoned French dressing; broil until lightly browned. (2) Dip in butter; alternate with quartered tomatoes or small cherry tomatoes; cook lightly.

Small Canned or Parboiled Potatoes. Dip in butter and broil until brown. After cooking they may be sprinkled with minced parsley or dill.

Small Parboiled Onions. Alternate with squares of green pepper and squares of bacon. Cook until brown.

Cubes of Parboiled Yams or Sweet Potatoes. Alternate with chunks of pineapple, and brush with butter before broiling.

Quartered Green Tomatoes. Wrap in bacon and cook until the bacon is crisp.

Small Zucchini. Cut in 1-inch slices, or use small green summer squash. Marinate in French dressing, and broil until tender. You may alternate the squash with onions, green pepper, or cherry tomatoes.

Sauces
and marinades

There is no mystery about the composition of barbecue sauces and marinades. They are simply a blend of three main ingredients: oil, seasonings, and a food acid such as lemon juice, vinegar, wine, or tomato juice. They are used to sharpen the flavor of meats, fowl, or fish, and to supply fat to meats that are lacking in natural oils. Some cooks believe that the food acids help to tenderize the meat.

Meats are soaked in marinades to flavor, and sometimes to tenderize them before they are put on the grill or spit. Some durable cuts profit from prolonged marinating—two or three days; most need only to be left for a few hours in the flavorful bath. Usually the marinade may also be used as a basting sauce.

Sauces are used primarily to supply flavor and oil to meats as they broil over charcoal. The liquid may be sloshed on with a basting brush or spooned over the meat. Some can be mixed with drippings to make gravy; some are served as is.

Steak Sauce

1 bunch green onions	1 teaspoon Worcestershire
3 cloves garlic, minced	1/2 teaspoon each of celery salt,
Butter for sautéing	garlic salt, onion salt, chili
1 cup catsup	powder, dry mustard, and
1/2 cup wine vinegar	dried mixed herbs

Cut up green onions and garlic in small pieces and sauté in butter until brown. Mix remaining ingredients in a bowl, then add the sautéed onions and garlic. Marinate steaks in this mixture for 3 hours before grilling.

Barney's Barbecue Sauce

1/4 cup vinegar	1/4 cube butter, melted
1/4 cup catsup	1/4 cup chopped onion
1/2 cup Worcestershire	1/2 teaspoon sugar
3/4 cup water	1/4 teaspoon chili powder
1 1/2 teaspoons dry mustard	Small clove garlic
3/4 teaspoon salt	Dash of red pepper

This sauce is good with spareribs, venison, or may be served over steamed wild rice. May be used as either marinade or basting sauce.

Special Barbecue Sauce

1/2 cup chopped shallots or	1/2 cup prepared English
green onions	mustard
1/4 cup olive oil	1/4 cup sugar
2 cups sauterne	Salt and pepper to taste
1 cup soy	1/4 cup chopped parsley
2 cups catsup	

Cook chopped shallots in olive oil for 5 minutes. Add sauterne and let reduce about half. Add all remaining ingredients except parsley. *Do not boil at any time.* Remove from fire, correct seasoning to taste, and add parsley. Makes about 1 quart sauce which can be kept in refrigerator until needed.

To use for barbecued meat: Rub meat with sauce and wait 10 minutes before broiling. Then broil meat slowly until tender.

Smoky Sauce

Add 1 tablespoon or more of liquid smoke, according to strength desired, to about 1 pint of your favorite barbecue sauce. Let meat or shish kebab stand in sauce for several hours or overnight to absorb flavors; use as basting sauce while the meat is barbecuing.

Lemon butter baste is applied to skewered scallops. Frequent basting is required for fatless foods such as this

Small bundle of bay leaves is used to baste lamb legs on spit. Fat cuts like these are basted mainly for seasoning

Thick Sauce

2 tablespoons lard or
   shortening
2 tablespoons flour
4 small cans (8 oz.) tomato
   sauce

1 tablespoon Worcestershire
5 tablespoons chili powder
   Few drops Tabasco
2 cloves (or powdered
   equivalent)

Heat fat until very hot. Add flour and stir until slightly browned. Add the rest of the ingredients and cook until thick. If too thick, add a little water, but it should not be a thin sauce.

Circle J Sauce

1 clove garlic, minced
1 small onion, minced
¾ teaspoon dry mustard
1 tablespoon grated fresh
   horseradish
1 tablespoon mixed minced
   herbs (thyme, marjoram,
   parsley)
2 tablespoons vinegar
3 cups water
¾ teaspoon salt

1 tablespoon A-1 sauce or
   Worcestershire
2/3 cup butter
½ cup catsup
½ teaspoon juice from a bottle
   of Tabasco peppers
2 teaspoons sugar
¾ teaspoon chili powder
¼ teaspoon black pepper,
   freshly ground

Combine all ingredients and cook slowly for 45 minutes. Use to baste meat or fish while cooking, or dip slices or chunks of hot cooked meat into the heated sauce before serving. Makes 3 cups.

Alki Point Sauce

2 tablespoons finely minced onion	1 medium sized tomato, diced
3 tablespoons finely minced green pepper	1/2 teaspoon salt
1 tablespoon butter	1/8 teaspoon pepper
1/2 cup water	1/4 teaspoon Kitchen Bouquet
	Dash of celery salt

Sauté onion and green pepper in the butter until they are golden brown. Add water, tomato, and seasonings. Bring to a boil. Simmer for 10 minutes, stirring frequently. Makes enough sauce for four meat servings.

Marinade

1 cup Zinfandel	2 or 3 sprigs rosemary
1 cup olive oil	2 or 3 sprigs thyme
2 or 3 cloves garlic	2 or 3 sprigs marjoram
1 bay leaf	

Mix all ingredients and set away in refrigerator. This preparation will keep indefinitely and will do for several barbecue occasions. The herbs may be strained out after the mixture is well flavored.

Cover steaks with the sauce and let stand from 6 to 36 hours before barbecuing. The sauce may also be used for basting when the meat is on the grill. Apply with a long stalk of celery, using the leaves on the end as a swab. The celery also adds flavor.

Basic Beef Sauce

2 cups tomato juice	1/4 cup catsup
1 teaspoon mustard	1/2 cup butter or margarine
1 tablespoon sugar	Few drops of Tabasco
3 tablespoons vinegar	3/4 teaspoon salt
2 teaspoons horseradish	1/2 teaspoon paprika
1 tablespoon Worcestershire	1/2 teaspoon freshly ground
1/4 cup grated onion	pepper
1 clove garlic, minced	

Simmer all ingredients for 30 minutes. For a different flavor, substitute meat stock for the tomato juice, or use half and half.

Sauce Jerez

1/4 pound process Cheddar
    cheese
1/2 cup sherry
1 teaspoon dry mustard

1/2 teaspoon seasoning salt
1/4 teaspoon paprika
Salt to taste

Melt cheese in double boiler and add wine, a little at a time, stirring constantly. When well blended, add seasonings, stirring thoroughly. Serve hot over steaks, lamb chops or other meat dishes.

Quentin Barbecue Sauce

1 good sized onion, finely
    chopped
3 or 4 cloves garlic, minced
1 sprig parsley, minced
2 cups catsup

1/2 cup wine vinegar
1 cup olive oil
2 tablespoons Worcestershire
    Freshly ground pepper
    to taste

Put ingredients in order given into a quart jar, cover and shake so ingredients will be well blended. Let stand 24 hours, shaking occasionally during the day. Use as basting sauce.

Garlic Sauce

1 clove garlic, minced

1/2 cup salad oil, olive oil or
    melted butter

Put the garlic to soak in oil the night before the barbecue. Or, if butter is used, melt and keep warm, with the clove of garlic floating in it about 2 hours before the meat is to be grilled. Use for basting grilled steaks or chops.

Easy-to-Make Sauce

1 can (8 oz.) tomato sauce
4 teaspoons Worcestershire
1/4 teaspoon each celery, onion,
    and garlic salt

4 tablespoons sherry
1 tablespoon wine vinegar
2 tablespoons olive oil
1 clove garlic, minced

Combine all ingredients. Place in a covered jar and let stand in refrigerator overnight, or at least for several hours.

Sandwich Sauce

This sauce is not for basting, but is served over barbecued meats and in sandwiches.

1 clove of garlic, minced	1/4 teaspoon marjoram
1 whole onion, minced	1 can (No. 2 1/2) tomatoes with
2 tablespoons oil	puree, sieved
2 teaspoons chili powder	1/4 cup vinegar
1 teaspoon dry mustard	1/2 teaspoon celery salt
2 bay leaves	

Cook the garlic and onion in oil about 5 minutes. Add the rest of the ingredients and simmer gently, stirring frequently, about 40 minutes or until mixture reaches desired thickness. Remove the bay leaves. It's ready for use or can be sealed in jars. If the sauce is heated before serving, the flavors of the meat and sauce are blended better. Makes about 2 cups.

Salsa (Steak Sandwich Sauce)

4 large onions	Freshly ground pepper
6 tomatoes	2 tablespoons wine vinegar
2 cans green chili, seeded	1/4 cup olive oil
Salt	

Mince onions, tomatoes, and green chili. Season with salt and pepper, add vinegar and olive oil. Let stand 2 hours before using.

Porterhouse Steak Sauce

1/2 cup olive oil	1 tablespoon paprika
3 tablespoons wine vinegar	1 teaspoon monosodium
1/2 tablespoon garlic salt	glutamate

Paint surfaces of steaks 1/2 hour before cooking and again just before putting them on the fire. This amount is sufficient for 4 good-sized porterhouse steaks.

Simple Steak Sauce

1 cup olive oil	Garlic slices to suit taste
1 cup wine or wine vinegar	1 tablespoon salt
2 good sized onions, grated	1 teaspoon freshly ground
or minced	pepper

Mix the oil and vinegar, then add the onion, garlic, salt and pepper. Pour into a pint fruit jar and stir until salt is dissolved. Let the mixture stand overnight, then stir well just before using.

Roasting Sauce

1/4 pound butter	1 tablespoon chili sauce
1 cup vinegar	1 teaspoon lemon juice
1/2 teaspoon dry mustard	2 lemon slices
1 tablespoon chopped onions	1 teaspoon brown sugar
2 tablespoons Worcestershire	1/2 pod red pepper, ground

Mix all ingredients together; put over low fire until the butter melts, then set where it will keep warm. Makes about 1½ cups.

Hamburger Sauce

For steaks or hamburgers. Enough for 6.

1 cube butter, melted	Grated onion or garlic as desired
1/2 cup olive oil	Juice of 1/2 lemon
1/2 cup catsup	Salt and freshly ground pepper
1 teaspoon prepared mustard	
Dash of Worcestershire	

Shake well. Use either as a marinade or a basting sauce.

Sauce for Steaks or Chops

1/2 cup peanut oil	1 large clove garlic, grated or crushed
1/4 cup wine vinegar	1 tablespoon each of brown sugar, salt, dry mustard, paprika, black pepper
1 or 2 tablespoons horseradish, freshly ground	Generous sprigs each of fresh rosemary, fresh sage, fresh thyme, parsley
1 cup hot water	
2 tablespoons Worcestershire	
2 tablespoons grated onion juice and pulp	
2 tablespoons chili sauce	

Simmer all ingredients together for about 15 minutes. Cool. Brush over patties while broiling; brush over both sides of chops or steak an hour before cooking. This sauce will keep satisfactorily for 2 weeks in the refrigerator.

Western Sauce

1 can (No. 2) tomatoes	2½ teaspoons salt
2 cups water	¼ teaspoon cayenne
1 can (6 oz.) tomato paste	¼ teaspoon Tabasco
2 dried chili peppers	2 teaspoons freshly ground
½ cup tomato catsup	black pepper
2 tablespoons sugar	1 large onion, chopped
2 teaspoons Worcestershire	1 clove garlic, chopped
2 teaspoons chili powder	2 bay leaves
Juice 2 lemons	½ pound butter
¼ cup wine vinegar	2 teaspoons dry mustard

Combine all ingredients and let simmer over low flame in covered pan for about 30 minutes. Strain through coarse sieve. This sauce can be kept several months in the refrigerator.

Southern Barbecue Sauce

1 quart cider vinegar	1½ tablespoons mixed whole
5 tablespoons Worcestershire	pickling spices
2 tablespoons A-1 sauce	1 bouillon cube
2 teaspoons salt	3 large slices unpeeled orange
1 tablespoon sugar	2 large slices unpeeled lemon
6 whole mint leaves	1 cup water
¼ teaspoon paprika	1 tablespoon catsup
4 shakes Tabasco	Sweet basil and oregano
½ teaspoon black pepper	to taste

Combine all ingredients. Put on the stove in an enamel or glass container, and simmer until the orange and lemon peel are pretty well cooked. Use this sauce on either pork or lamb. Excellent for basting spareribs.

Ham Sauce

½ teaspoon black pepper	1 tablespoon sugar
½ teaspoon salt	½ cup vinegar
1 teaspoon dry mustard	1 egg

Mix dry ingredients, add vinegar and slightly beaten egg. Heat until egg is set, stirring constantly, but do not boil. When slightly thickened, add:

½ cup catsup	½ cup tart jelly (grape or currant)

Stir until jelly has melted. If the sauce curdles, strain but never boil.

Basic Pork Sauce

1½ cups tomato sauce
½ cup water
1/3 cup vinegar
1/3 cup brown sugar
2 tablespoons butter or
   margarine

1 teaspoon smoked salt
1 teaspoon ginger
½ teaspoon paprika
1 small onion, minced

Simmer all ingredients for 30 minutes.

Venison Sauce

Chop the following fresh herbs: 1 teaspoon each of marjoram, rosemary, sage, thyme. Add:

1 pint salad oil
2/3 pint wine vinegar
2 tablespoons Worcestershire

1/3 cup parsley
Garlic (let your conscience
   be your guide, but plenty)

Mix thoroughly, adding salt and pepper to taste, and let the mixture stand overnight. Dip the venison chops or steaks in the sauce and broil, turning once or twice, until medium done.

Basic Lamb Sauce

¾ cup sherry
1 slice lemon
1 sprig parsley, minced
2 tablespoons olive oil
1 teaspoon grated onion
1 teaspoon salt

½ teaspoon pepper
1 sprig each fresh rosemary
   and oregano, minced, or
   ½ teaspoon each dried
   herbs

Let stand for several hours to blend.

Lamb Shish Kebab Sauce

1 can (6 oz.) tomato paste
½ cup olive oil
1 cup honey
1 cup dry white table wine

2 cloves garlic, crushed
½ teaspoon each crushed rosemary and oregano
1 teaspoon salt

Mix all ingredients. Thread squares of lamb (cut from shoulder or leg) on skewers, pour over sauce, and let stand a few minutes before cooking. (You can marinate lamb in your favorite wine-and-oil marinade first and use 1 cup of the marinade instead of the dry white wine.) Barbecue about 20 minutes, basting often with sauce during the process. Sauce is ample for about 3½ pounds of meat on 7 large skewers—to serve 7.

Herb Sauce for Lamb

This recipe, using garden herbs for unusual flavor, was given to a *Sunset* reader by the great-grandson of one of the first Spanish governors of California.

1 small onion or half a large one	12 fresh mint leaves
3 cloves garlic	1/4 cup vinegar
2 sprigs rosemary	1/2 cup water

Chop the onion and garlic fine and add the rosemary and mint leaves which have been crushed or chopped. Then add the vinegar and water and let the mixture stand overnight.

When ready to barbecue steaks or chops, brush them thoroughly with the sauce, using a bunch of mint leaves for a brush. As the meat cooks, baste occasionally with more of the liquid. If still more sauce is desired, pass a cruet of it when serving.

Marinade and Basting Sauce for Lamb

1 cup olive oil	1 teaspoon mint (fresh or dried)
1/2 cup red wine vinegar (flavored with garlic or eschalot, if desired)	1 teaspoon freshly ground pepper
1 teaspoon thyme	1/2 teaspoon salt
1 teaspoon monosodium glutamate	1/2 teaspoon paprika

Mix all ingredients. Marinate lamb for at least 2 hours before barbecuing. Baste frequently with sauce while cooking in a Chinese smoke oven or broiling over charcoal. Makes enough sauce for about 6 chops or a 3 to 5-pound roast.

Kebab Sauce

1 can (10 1/2 oz.) condensed tomato soup	Worcestershire
Oil or shortening	Paprika
1 teaspoon dry mustard	Pepper
1 teaspoon sugar (brown or granulated)	1 onion, chopped fine
1 teaspoon salt	1 large clove garlic, chopped fine
2 teaspoons chili powder	Pinch rosemary leaves
3 to 4 tablespoons wine or vinegar	1 tablespoon liquid smoke

Empty contents of can of tomato soup into a saucepan; fill can about three-fourths full of water, and add enough shortening or oil to bring water to top of the can; pour into saucepan. Add mustard, sugar, salt, chili powder, and wine or vinegar; Worcestershire, paprika, and pepper to taste; chopped onion, chopped garlic, mashed well with a tiny bit of shortening; rosemary leaves, and liquid smoke.

Heat to boiling and cook for about 5 minutes, or until all ingredients are well blended. Makes about 2¾ cups of sauce. May be made in quantity and stored in the refrigerator.

Chicken or Turkey Wine Sauce

1 cup white table wine	1 teaspoon salt
¼ cup olive oil	¼ teaspoon paprika
2 tablespoons butter or margarine	2 teaspoons fresh rosemary, minced
1 medium sized onion, minced	1 teaspoon parsley, minced
1 clove garlic, crushed	Freshly ground pepper

Simmer all ingredients for 15 minutes. Use as basting sauce.

Citrus Sauce for Chicken

The citrus-soy-honey-butter combination is most effective if you baste just as often as possible. There is no salt in the recipe because it tends to dry out the chicken. Salt to taste after cooking is completed.

¼ cup butter	¼ cup chopped parsley (not too fine)
1 cup orange juice (as you drink, not concentrated)	¼ cup soy
Juice of 1 large lemon (3 tablespoons)	1 tablespoon dry mustard
¼ cup honey	2 medium sized garlic cloves mashed (optional)

Combine all sauce ingredients. Chickens should be of small fryer size, split, with wings and necks removed. Place chicken on grill and cook *very* slowly and baste with the sauce constantly. Cook chicken halves, cavity side down, for 40 to 45 minutes. Turn and cook meat side down for an additional 7 to 10 minutes. Recipe makes enough sauce for 2 chickens of 2 to 2½-pound size—sufficient to serve 4.

Poultry Marinade

This marinade will flavor 8 fryer halves (1¾ to 2½ pounds) or cut-up young turkeys.

2 to 3 cloves garlic
8 heaping teaspoons quick-cure salt (obtainable in rural localities)
1 level teaspoon each of thyme, celery salt, black pepper
2 heaping teaspoons dry mustard
½ teaspoon each of poultry seasoning, fresh grated ginger root, monosodium glutamate
¾ cup sauterne
1 cup red wine vinegar
Olive oil

Mince garlic, put in bowl, add salt and crush together. Add other spices, then wine and vinegar. Do not add oil until ready to cook. Stir thoroughly until salt is dissolved, or shake well in covered jar.

Put liquid in large bowl, dip each piece of fowl into it, place fowl in baking dish or flat pan, skin side down. Stir balance of marinade and pour over fowl. Let stand 2 to 3 hours, then turn fowl over and let stand again for 2 to 3 hours.

When ready to barbecue, pour marinade off fowl. Add olive oil to marinade in an amount equal to about ¼ the volume of marinade remaining. Stir thoroughly, brush each piece of fowl with mixture before placing on grill. Paint again each time fowl is turned.

Variation:

A simplified version of this sauce is used to flavor steaks.

8 teaspoons quick-cure salt
1 teaspoon black pepper
¾ cup sauterne
1 cup red wine vinegar
½ teaspoon monosodium glutamate
Olive oil

Mix ingredients together, and soak steaks for 2 to 3 hours. Remove steaks from marinade, add olive oil equal to about ¼ the volume and baste steaks while grilling.

Cowboy Barbecue Sauce

This sauce is sufficient for 8 to 10 chickens or the same amount, by weight, of meat.

2 cups butter or margarine	1/4 teaspoon cayenne
5 cups water	1 tablespoon each Worcestershire, Tabasco, and black pepper
1/2 cup vinegar	
2 teaspoons dry mustard	
2 tablespoons sugar	1 medium sized onion, chopped fine
1 1/2 tablespoons each of salt, chili powder, and paprika	1 clove garlic, minced

Mix all ingredients together and simmer for 30 minutes. Soak meat in sauce before broiling and pour over meat as served.

Simple Sauce for Chicken

Let chicken stand for 2 or 3 hours at room temperature in a mixture of:

2 parts olive oil	Salt and pepper
1 part wine vinegar	Generous pinch each of tarragon, thyme, and chopped parsley
1 medium sized onion, minced	
1 clove garlic, minced	

Use same mixture to baste chicken during cooking.

Duck Sauce

1/2 cube butter or margarine	Juice and chopped peel of 1/2 lemon
2 tablespoons olive oil	
2 large onions, chopped	1 sprig fresh rosemary
2 cloves garlic	1/2 dozen sage leaves
1 large green pepper, chopped	1/2 teaspoon monosodium glutamate
1/2 cup celery, chopped	1 pint white or red wine

Melt the butter in frying pan with olive oil, then add all the remaining ingredients except the wine. Sauté until mixture is soft and the onions a golden brown. Just before serving the ducks, add the wine to the mixture, and bring to a boil. Pour over the ducks and serve.

Marinade for Poultry or Game

1 part Italian Vermouth	1 part olive oil

Combine wine and olive oil, mixing well. Mix thoroughly each time you baste.

Soy Marinade for Fish

Marinate fish for 4 to 5 hours in a mixture of equal parts of soy sauce and water, with crushed garlic to taste. Garlic and soy sauce make a combination used frequently by the Japanese in their fish cookery. For added piquancy squeeze a little lemon or lime over the fish while they're cooking.

Fish Sauce

2 cups meat or chicken stock	1 tablespoon Worcestershire
1 tablespoon soy sauce	1/4 cup catsup
1 tablespoon lemon juice	1 teaspoon paprika

Simmer all ingredients for 30 minutes. Pour over fish before serving.

Fish Marinade

1/4 cup soy sauce	1/4 cup salad oil (use less oil if your fish is a fat one)
1/4 cup bourbon or 1/2 cup sherry wine	1/2 teaspoon monosodium glutamate
1 clove garlic, crushed	

Combine soy sauce, bourbon or sherry, well crushed garlic, olive oil, and monosodium glutamate. Let mixture stand to blend flavors.

Smoke cooking

The tantalizing flavor and rich mahogany color of smoke-cooked foods are tempting many an outdoor cook to try out the "new" technique.

Smoke cooking borrows much from the centuries-old method of the Chinese oven, which roasts with indirect heat from a wood fire, and it also picks up some modern tricks used in commercial smoke preservation of meat and fish.

In hot smoke cooking, a wide variety of foods may be cooked in a 250° to 400° oven filled with aromatic smoke. Although cold smoke curing can be done in a smoke oven, hot smoke cooking is the simplest way to impart a mild smoke flavor to meat, fish, and poultry.

Whether you buy a commercial "smoker," or build a traditional Chinese oven or one of its homemade cousins, you will enter a new realm of taste experience.

Smoke Control

If your oven is designed to burn wood, you can get a consistent, natural smoke by using green, freshly cut wood or by soaking dry wood in a bucket of water before placing it on a hot bed of coals. If you are limited to charcoal as a fuel, or want to increase the quantity of smoke, add chips of specially prepared aromatic wood, fresh prunings, or hardwood sawdust or shavings soaked in water.

Every smoke enthusiast has his favorite wood—only hard-and-fast rule is never to use pine or any soft wood that gives off a resinous, sooty smoke.

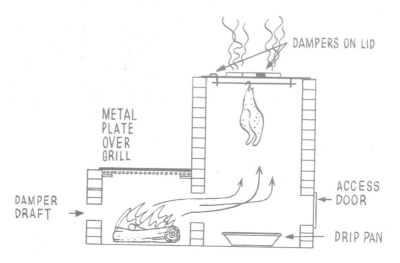

This drawing shows the elements of a simple smoke oven. The cooking food hangs in a chamber away from direct heat of the fire. All drippings fall away from the coals. The draft is controlled at the top and at the firebox opening. Hot smoke (from green wood or wet chips) fills the cooking chamber

What to Smoke Cook

There seems to be no limit to the foods that can be prepared by this method. The only real limits are those imposed by the design of your oven.

Timing varies with each food. In a Chinese oven with no direct heat, times are comparable to those for ordinary oven cookery—perhaps a little shorter. With a heat source directly below, you have to avoid charring the underside of the food.

Ducks, chickens, turkeys, and ribs are hung from hooks over bars built in top of oven. Sheet metal lid fits on the top, has hinged section for draft control

All important principles of traditional Chinese oven are followed in the plans for this Western version. Food can be hung from hooks at the top, or placed on a metal grill inside the oven door

You can best judge timing by experience, and in the beginning, by using a good thermometer. For roasts and heavier cuts of meat, your best bet is a standard meat thermometer. Air temperature thermometers are recommended by some experts, scorned by others. For smaller pieces of meat, you'll have to develop a practiced eye—and slice off an occasional sample.

Perhaps the most versatile, all-round smoke cooker is the masonry Chinese oven—similar to the one shown on this page—because of several general reasons:

- You can do any kind of open fire cooking from low temperature cold smoking to high temperature "flash broiling."
- You can hang great quantities of food from the top of the chimney-like oven for large-party entertaining.

Square rack holds three tiers of skewers loaded with shish kebab. The direction of skewers is alternated. Rack is lowered into the chimney of smoke oven for cooking. Since heat surrounds the food, there is no need to rotate skewers

The Rube Goldberg-like smoke oven on the left is an inexpensive alternative to the larger masonry Chinese oven. One difficulty—occasional cracking of the flue tile—can be minimized by starting fires slowly, especially in cold weather. You will need 40 bricks, set up dry; a portable oven obtainable through a hardware store or mail order house (you will have to cut the metal bottom out); a 13 by 8-inch clay flue tile; a 14 by 24-inch sheet of 3/16-inch steel. Heat is controlled by the brick "dampers" at the front. Smoke from fire circulates through the bottomless oven and escapes around door and sides

- You can maintain an even temperature for indefinite periods without disturbing food that is cooking.
- You can use any kind of fuel and you can add it conveniently whenever additional heat is required.
- Your fire is indirect—grease drippings can't fall on the coals to cause unwanted flames or a greasy smoke.
- You can control smoke flavor by adding smoke-producing fuel as often as you wish. Some true Chinese oven experts use dry wood and prefer no smoke at all; others stand by with a bucket of wet sawdust and make the air blue with a moist, aromatic smoke.

Unlimited cooking possibilities

There's no limit to the variety of meats and fish that you can smoke-roast. Not only will the food have a wonderful smoky flavor, but also, as a consequence of the slow cooking process, meat and fish retain their natural juices and flavors.

A 30-gallon oil drum forms chimney of this smoke oven. The metal firebox is lined with insulating asbestos. Periodic addition of aromatic wood chips to the bed of coals maintains constant, smoky heat. Added features include a built-in thermometer, folding counter, and wheels. A drip bucket hangs on the spout at the bottom of the oven

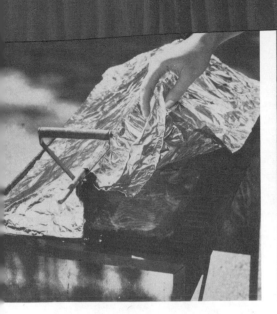 

An improvised tent of aluminum foil can substitute for a hood on a conventional portable barbecue. Throw green wood, twigs, sawdust on coals for smoke

Commercial cookers are clean, shiny, convenient to use. Most have rubber-tired wheels, and many have an electric spit attachment and a built-in counter

You should keep your fire low enough so that the temperature in the oven stays between 300° and 350°.

Fish

Both salmon steaks and fresh trout are delicious cooked in a smoke oven. Either needs only a good rubbing with salt and pepper and an occasional basting with equal parts of melted butter and hot water. Use a good white wine with the butter if you prefer, but the smoke flavor is more pronounced with only the butter-water sauce. Time: 30 minutes for small trout, 45 minutes for inch-thick salmon steaks. Do not try to turn the fish, as it will crumble.

Save several of the smoked trout (if you can) and chill them in the refrigerator. Boned and cut in small pieces, they make mouth-watering hors d'oeuvres.

Chicken

Rub well with salt, pepper, brown sugar, and tarragon vinegar. Turn and baste the chicken occasionally with a mixture of butter and warm water for moist, even cooking. Smoking will impart a golden-orange color to the chicken unlike any you've seen before. Time: 2½ to 3 hours.

Two Smoke Barrels

1

Elegantly appointed oak barrel has a copper lining and an electric spit. Handle, lower right, operates a winch to lower or raise the fire pan inside the oven. Barrel rests on a plywood disk, which rolls on roller skate wheels

Angle brackets screwed inside barrel support expanded metal grill. You place fire pan on winch-operated platform. A Japanese hibachi is ideal for fire pan. Start fire outside the barrel, place inside when coals are just right

Steak

Smoked steak, of course, will be different from what you're accustomed to. Cooked through, it will still be moist; and it will have the handsome tinge of brick color peculiar to smoked meat.

Prepare a large (at least an inch thick) sirloin. Rub both sides of the steak with soy sauce, then sprinkle with salt and pepper. Turn the steak and baste it occasionally with a warm mixture of half butter and half water. After steak is roasted, slice it into separate portions for serving. Time: about 2½ hours for medium. But check it sooner if this long cooking period makes you suspicious.

Spareribs

The cooking procedure and time for spareribs are the same as for steak.

Chinese Ribs

2 sides pork spareribs
1/4 cup soy
1 teaspoon pepper
4 tablespoons honey

1/4 cup sherry
2 teaspoons monosodium glutamate

Marinate whole sides of the spareribs in a mixture of the soy, pepper, honey, sherry, and monosodium glutamate for at least 30 minutes. Remove the ribs from the marinade and allow to dry thoroughly.

Hang the ribs from the top of a moderate Chinese oven for 1¼ to 1½ hours. The closer you place the ribs to the actual fire, the more carefully you have to watch for charring.

Chinese-Oven Pig (Sui Gee)

Take a 15 to 20-pound pig, remove most of the shoulder bones, and split the backbone from the inside, taking care not to cut the outer skin. Replace the shoulder blade and pelvis bone with

On this barrel cooker, a much simpler version than that shown on opposite page, salmon fillets, other loose-textured foods are placed in hardware cloth tray on removable rods. Note the notches for rods in supporting bar

Rods provide hanging space for many sides of ribs. Heavy gauge steel wire is bent to make simple hooks. Hooks are easier to retrieve from oven if made with an extra bend for a finger hold. Barrel mounted on rubber-tired wheels

Chinese Approach
to Smoke Cookery

If you have admired the shiny, reddish-brown, cooked ducks that hang in the Chinatown markets, you might like Peking duck method with chicken, turkey, goose, duck, or other fowl. Peking duck is not a species, but a method of preparing, roasting, serving. To prepare turkey, sew up neck tightly, hang bird from a nail. Paint with mixture of 1 pound honey, 2 tablespoons water, 1/3 cup soy; let dry. Repeat 5 to 10 times. If basting can be managed conveniently, reserve ½ cup of mixture for this purpose. Before placing bird in smoke oven, fill cavity with mixture of ¼ cup baste, 2 tablespoons chopped

ginger root, ½ cup sherry, ¼ teaspoon anise, 1 chopped onion. 11-pound turkey should roast for 3½ hours at 300°

bamboo sticks so the pig won't lose its shape. Rub salt and pepper and a barbecue sauce with a catsup base in the cavities, wire the pig, and hang in the oven which has been preheated so the masonry walls are very hot. Put the cover in place and cook for ½ hour.

Remove the pig and puncture holes through the skin with an ice pick over the entire surface of the animal to allow some of the fat and juices to escape. Wash with hot water to which a little honey has been added, return to the oven and cook until done, usually 1 to 2 hours. Seal lid of oven with wet sacks to retain heat.

Marinade for Chinese-Oven Chicken

2 tablespoons soy
1 cup boysenberry or logan-
    berry jelly
2 tablespoons lemon juice

1½ teaspoons powdered ginger
½ teaspoon freshly ground
    pepper

Mix together soy, jelly, lemon juice, ginger, and pepper. Heat gently in a saucepan until jelly is melted. Marinate chicken—the inside as well as the outside—in this mixture for about 1 hour,

Salmon Smoke

Trussed salmon rest on expanded metal grill 3 feet above fire. Hot fire was "killed" with green wood when fish were ready for cooking. Fish were cleaned, scaled, salted inside and out 5 hours before cooking. "Cradle" is made of green sticks tied with heavy cord, braced with cross sticks. Use wide strips of butcher paper staked to ground for smoke "tent." A 12-pound salmon needs 5 to 6 hours cooking. Turn every 30 minutes. During last 30 minutes, toss a little dry wood on fire for more heat. Test for doneness. When done, skin fish, cut the meat crosswise down to the backbone, salt, lift off the backbone and salt the other side

then hang in a Chinese oven. About 10 minutes before you expect to remove the chicken from the oven, lift it out, brush it liberally with marinade, and return it for the final cooking.

This quantity of marinade should be ample for two chickens.

Surprised Squab

4 tender, fat squabs
3 tablespoons soy
1/4 teaspoon monosodium glutamate
1 tablespoon brown sugar
3 tablespoons Scotch whisky
   Salt and pepper to taste
1 medium sized onion, chopped
4 squab gizzards, sliced

3 tablespoons butter
2 cups diced white bread
3 medium sized cooked shrimp or 6 dried Chinese shrimp, broken in small pieces
6 water chestnuts, sliced
1 cup milk
1 teaspoon salt
1/4 teaspoon pepper
   Salad oil

Marinate the squabs in a mixture of the soy, monosodium glutamate, brown sugar, whisky, salt and pepper for about 1 hour. Brush the inside and outside of each bird with this mixture several times during the hour.

Fry the onion and gizzards in 1 tablespoon of the butter until brown. Add the remaining 2 tablespoons of melted butter and mix with the diced bread, shrimps, water chestnuts, milk, salt, and pepper.

Fit this stuffing inside each bird, and sew up the openings. Skewer together each pair of legs or tie with light wire. Brush skins with oil and hang in a moderate (300° to 400°) Chinese oven for about 1 hour and 15 minutes. Brush the skins with salad oil once again during the cooking process. Serve one juicy squab per person.

Salmon Lovers' Salmon

Whole salmon, 6 to 8 pounds
1 cup lemon juice
1 cup dry white table wine
2 teaspoons salt

1/2 teaspoon pepper
1 medium sized onion, chopped fine

Have the salmon cleaned and filleted with the skin left intact. Marinate both fillets in the lemon juice, wine, salt, and pepper mixture for at least 30 minutes. Lay the salmon, skin side down, on a piece of hardware cloth and spread the onion over the top. Bake in a very slow Chinese oven (200° to 250°) about 45 minutes.

Smoked Salmon Hors d'oeuvres

Cut a salmon fillet carefully into finger-size pieces, including 3 or 4 "leaves" of meat in each piece. Marinate for 30 minutes or more in a lemon or wine base marinade that includes a small amount of salad oil. Place pieces of salmon on a sheet of aluminum foil and cook in a very slow, very smoky Chinese oven until done to your taste. These hors d'oeuvres are neat enough to serve hot or cold right from the aluminum "platter." The small size of each piece allows it to take on an especially smoky flavor.

Firepit barbecuing

In the early days of the West, the science of cooking underground was certainly known to many of the Indians and to the white scouts and hunters and trappers who roamed the country. It could make their deer or buffalo taste mighty good, if they were in the mood for digging the pit, tending the fire, and waiting patiently for the meat to be done. However, the ones who seemed to take to this method most readily were the cattle ranchers and their cowboys. It is such an excellent way to cook mountainous chunks of beef— and they had the beef.

Westerners still favor this method for cooking beef, especially as such all-out community occasions as round-ups, rodeos, fairs, and farmers' picnics. It works well with other meats, and it's famous with beans. And, most important to the way we live today, you can do pit cookery in a small way just as successfully as you can with a whole side of beef. (Use one of the cheaper grades of meat for your first experiment.)

Essentially, cooking underground is a primitive version of roasting meat in an oven, with two important exceptions: 1) You can't

1 *Fire started at 6:30 A.M. Pit is 4 by 7 by 3½ feet deep, bottom covered with brick, for 155 pounds beef (serves 250) in 20 separate 6 to 10-pound rolls. The fire burned 6 hours, used ½ cord of oak*

2 *Each roll gets ¼ cup of special seasoning: 1 pound each garlic and onion salt, large bottle chili powder, small can of dry mustard, ½ package poultry seasoning, ½ small can pepper, 2 tbsps. sugar*

peek into your "oven" to see whether the meat is done, or you may destroy the effectiveness of your coals. 2) Because the meat is tightly wrapped, it is really steam-cooked under pressure rather than roasted.

Steam-cooking keeps the meat moist while it is in the pit but is no guarantee against overcooking. It doesn't prevent overcooked meat from drying out and losing its flavor as soon as it is exposed to the air. In pit barbecuing, meat doesn't get the kind of searing that seals in juices when you roast it in the oven or cook it over an open fire.

How do you control the process? You can't read dials on the oven or on a meat thermometer. You have to control the cooking by the way you handle the fire and by your timing. The important elements are these: 1) size of the pit, 2) kind of wood, 3) length of time the fire burns before you put on the meat, 4) preparation of the meat for cooking underground, 5) covering of the meat and the fire, 6) cooking time.

Size of the Pit

The experts on pit barbecuing don't agree among themselves as

3 *Final additions to each roll: 2 tablespoons Kitchen Bouquet, 2 teaspoons salt, 2 twigs rosemary, 2 bay leaves. Then wrap in 2-foot square of parchment paper, previously soaked in water*

4 *Parchment-wrapped rolls are then put in burlap bags, pre-soaked in water, tied with baling wire—tightened with pliers. Ready to go on the fire, rolls are wet with hose—but not soaked*

to the proper size of the pit. Actually, you can figure out the best size for your own operation if you understand the method.

Length and width. Obviously, these dimensions should be large enough so you can spread the meat out on the coals, in one large package or several small ones. In addition, there should be a little extra space all around the meat, so that heat from the outer coals will cook the outside edges of the meat. On a small-scale

5 *Meat goes on coals at 12:15 P.M., to cook for next 5 hours. It must go on fast so sacks won't burn (these are used over and over). Covered with short pieces of corrugated, galvanized iron*

6 *Dirt is shoveled on fast to a depth of about 1 foot. One man stays in pit to stamp down dirt (wears heavy shoes, jacket to protect arms). At 5:10 P.M. dirt is removed and rolls taken out*

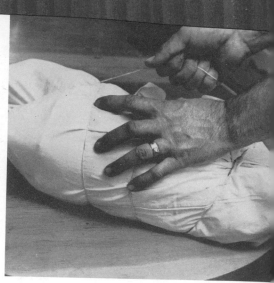

Metal syringe used to inject marinade along bone of lamb leg. Marinade: ½ cup each olive oil, vinegar; garlic, mint, sage, rosemary, summer savory, thyme

1

After marinade has been injected all along the bone of the lamb, meat is next wrapped in foil and then in a tea towel. Package is then tied with cord

2

job, you might cheat a little on the outside edge and make the pit about 1½ feet wide. For easy handling of the meat and general convenience, a 3-foot width is about maximum. Length can be anything required by the quantity of the meat.

Depth. Here you just add up the thickness of each layer you intend to put in the pit.

Many experts like to line the bottom (and sometimes part way up the sides) with bricks or with large round stones, which should be hard and dry, without crevices or porous sections holding water that might later make the rock explode under steam pressure.

When the pit is ready for cooking, the first thing you must add is the bed of coals; recommended depths range from 1 to 2 feet (depends on cooking time you favor). Next comes the meat; some put it right on the coals and others bank the fire and protect the meat from possible burning with about an inch of preheated dry sand. Finally comes the layer of dirt (right on the meat package or on a cover of metal or canvas); recommended depth is about 1 foot.

Add up these figures and you get a depth of about 2½ to 5 feet. It varies according to the depth of the bed of coals, the size

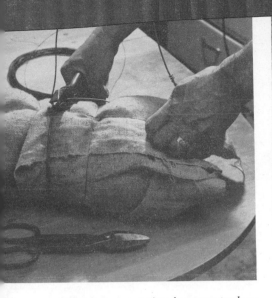 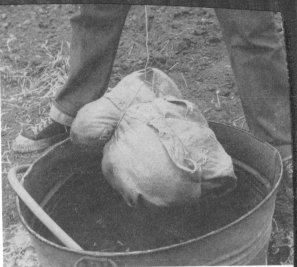

The outer wrapping for meat package is clean burlap sacking. You can secure it with light wire. A long piece of soft but heavier wire will serve as a handle

3

Each package is dunked in water, then put on the coals. The package is then covered with dirt, with the wire handle protruding above to make removal easy

4

of the meat packages, and, if you use a cover, whether you put it right on the meat or a few inches above it. (If you use galvanized iron, burn off the coating beforehand so it won't add an undesirable flavor to the meat.)

If you cook a pot of beans underground, you can use a smaller, shallower pit. The bed of coals may be as little as 6 inches deep, although a little extra depth won't matter.

Kind of Wood

The aim is to prepare a bed of coals of the approximate size and consistency of charcoal. All the pieces of wood should be burning or be thoroughly charred. Any uncharred pieces should be removed before the meat is placed on top.

Wood has to be fairly hard if it is to burn slowly enough to pile up a bed of coals. Anything as soft and fast-burning as pine is likely to leave ashes and very little else.

Favorite woods for this purpose include oak, alder, hickory, mesquite, ironwood, and the wood from most orchard trees—walnut, pecan, apple, orange, lemon. Needless to say, the wood should be thoroughly dry. It burns best if pieces aren't more than about 4 inches thick.

How Long Should the Fire Burn?

When you stoke your preliminary fire, you are really heating up an oven—the bottom and sides of your pit—so that the stored heat will continue to cook for the next several hours. The principle is very much like that of the igloo-shaped Mexican oven, in which you build your fire, then scrape it all out and do your cooking with the heat stored in the walls.

In the pit barbecue, you should keep replenishing the fire until the bed of coals reaches the desired depth. Each expert has his own timing on this step, but the majority would agree that 3 to 6 hours should be enough to develop a 1 to 2-foot depth of coals. Less than 3 hours may not pre-heat your "oven" enough; more than 6 hours may get it too hot, and you'll probably be consuming more wood than necessary.

Preparing the Meat

Standard practice is to wrap the chunks of meat in one or more layers of closely woven white cloth, parchment, or foil, and tie with twine; then wrap in one or more thicknesses of burlap and secure with wire. Each package is sprinkled or doused quickly in water before it goes on the coals.

Before wrapping, you can use any of the seasonings you might use with a roast. You can sprinkle the meat with liquid and dry seasonings. You can inject marinades with a syringe. Some like to put a little fat in each package of meat. Others always add a bouquet of herbs.

The traditional large-scale barbecue calls for whole quarters or whole sides of beef. But without a whole corps of meat cutters on duty, it is difficult to carve such huge pieces fast enough to serve the meat while it is still hot. For this reason many now prefer to bone the meat beforehand and tie in reasonably small rolls that can be carved fast and easily. You can keep each piece wrapped until the cutter is ready to go to work on it. This method is definitely best for any family-size pit barbecue.

Covering the Pit

The most primitive method is to pile the layer of dirt right on the meat packages—and do it fast before they have a chance to burn. A good idea here is to wrap a length of thick but soft wire around each package and let it stick up above the layer of dirt; you'll have no trouble pulling out each piece of meat and won't have to grapple for it with either a shovel or pitchfork.

For a more sanitary job, and especially if you'd like to use your burlap again for the same purpose, put a cover over the meat before throwing on the dirt. Canvas is used occasionally, but by far the most popular covering is thick sheet iron or corrugated galvanized iron (with the coating well burned off).

Some improvise a frame inside the pit in order to get the cover close to the meat. Others put pipes or rods across the top of the pit to support the cover; then they mound up the dirt on top.

In either case, work fast. Shovel dirt until you see no smoke or steam escaping. Some prefer to stamp on the dirt as it is being piled up. Others use a little water and seal the top with mud.

About every half hour, make an inspection to see that no steam is escaping. If it is, cover with dirt and stamp it down.

Cooking Time

Here is the supreme test of artistry. You have to know your fire and what it will do. You also have to gauge time by the size of your pieces of meat, much as you gauge oven cooking times by the size of your roast. Generally, meat in 6 to 10-pound pieces will require about 5 hours cooking time; in 20-pound pieces, 8 to 10 hours; hindquarters of beef (100 to 150 pounds, dressed), 15 to 18 hours; pots of beans, 4 to 6 hours.

The theory is that if your preliminary firing is right, the heat will subside after the first few hours of cooking is done. You do have some latitude, but don't trust this theory too far.

Before your first trial, study the step-by-step directions in the various recipes in this chapter. You'll have to do some experimenting and adjusting to fit these directions to your cooking job.

It's worth noting that the most reliable experts in this field are not improvisers at all. After trial and error, they've learned exactly what to do (pit, fire, and timing) with a certain quantity of meat. They have developed a set routine and they know it well, and they don't mind repeating it over and over again.

Barbecue for a Crowd

20 pounds beef shoulder roast (needn't be an expensive grade)
Salt
Garlic salt

3 large onions
2 tablespoons Worcestershire
2 or 3 bay leaves
Pinch of oregano

Dig a pit 2 feet wide, 3 feet long, and about 2½ feet deep. Have enough wood on hand to fill the pit at least 3 times. Start the fire about 15 hours before serving time. Keep adding wood as needed until the fire has been burning about 3 hours.

Meanwhile, salt the meat generously, then add a few dashes of garlic salt. Cut up the onions and scatter them over the meat. Dash the meat with the Worcestershire. Add bay leaves and oregano. Wait until the fire has burned down to a bed of hot coals about a foot thick.

For the last stage, you need: aluminum foil; a 10-foot length of butcher paper; heavy twine; 2 burlap sacks; wire; 1 or more sheets galvanized iron (enough to cover the pit); 2 pipes about 3 feet long.

Put all pieces of meat together and wrap in aluminum foil as a single package, folding edges to retain juices. Then wrap in 3 or 4 thicknesses of heavy butcher paper and tie with heavy twine. Place package in a burlap sack; then wrap another sack around it and tie with wire.

Dip package in a tub of water, or wet thoroughly with a hose. Drop directly on the coals (when ready), place pipes across the pit, and cover with galvanized iron. Waste no time in covering the top with at least a foot of dirt, until you see no signs of smoke or heat. Sprinkle with a hose. Check again in 30 minutes; if dry spots have appeared, shovel on more dirt.

Meat will be ready to serve in 10 to 12 hours. Makes 20 to 30 servings.

Imu Cookery

Prepare the firepit by digging a hole about 2 feet deep, lining the bottom and sides with medium sized stones. Do not use sandstone or wet rocks from a creek bed. Build a good fire of wood in the pit, and put a few more rocks in it. When it burns down to coals, remove the extra rocks and the coals and save them for future use. Line the pit with fresh grass or leaves. If you use leaves, be sure that they are not bitter because this would impart an unpleasant flavor to your food. Taste them to be sure they are sweet.

Season your meat and wrap it securely in aluminum foil or plain wrapping paper. Do the same with your potatoes (either peeled or in their jackets, as you prefer), and other vegetables, wrapping them individually and securely. Carrots, turnips, onions, squash—all these and many others are delicious when cooked by this method.

Place your wrapped meat and vegetables on the bottom of the pit, cover with a thick layer of grass or leaves, and cover with the hot stones. Now replace the still-hot coals on top of the stones. And, last but not least, cover with the earth from the original excavation, making sure that it is airtight so that there is no steam or smoke escaping.

After 3 or 4 hours, depending upon the size and type of your meat, you are ready for a piping hot dinner.

Bean-hole beans

3 pounds dried beans (any kind you prefer)	½ cup brown sugar
	2 cans (8 oz.) tomato sauce
¾ pound bacon or salt pork	1 tablespoon salt

Dig a hole twice as wide as your kettle and deep enough so top will be at least 6 inches below surface. Arrange rocks on bottom and sides. Build a fire and keep it burning for at least 2 hours.

Wash beans—or drain if previously soaked overnight. Place in large kettle and fill about ¾ full of water. Bring to a boil and boil 15 minutes. Cut up bacon or salt pork, add to beans; boil for another 15 minutes. Stir in brown sugar, tomato sauce, salt.

Remove all burning embers from hole. Put lid on kettle, wrap it thickly in newspapers, then wrap whole package in two thicknesses of wet burlap. Spread hot coals evenly, then cover with ½ inch dirt or sand. Set wrapped kettle in hole; cover with at least 6 inches dirt or sand. Dig out pot after 6 hours, serve. Serves 12.

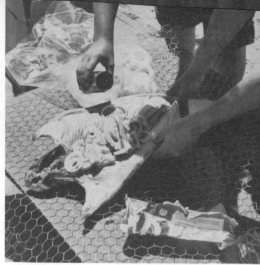

1 *To bake a 10-pound salmon, dig pit and line with rocks. Burn fire 3 hours while you prepare corn (remove silk, tie the husks); wash and prick potatoes; wash carrots, season to taste, wrap in foil*

2 *Gather and wash seaweed. Clean salmon, scale, remove head. Stuff fish with 1 sliced onion, 1 sliced cucumber, ½ cup sliced celery. Place 4 bacon strips over stuffing. Sprinkle with salt, pepper*

King Salmon

A 40-pound king salmon will serve about 20. To pit-barbecue a king salmon, first dig a 3-foot pit in the usual manner. A 40-pound king salmon will probably measure about 40 inches in length, so you'll need a pit 4 or 5 feet long, depending on the size of the fish. Build a fire of hardwood, and let it burn down until it forms a bed of coals 8 to 12 inches deep.

Meanwhile, place the fish on a large sheet of parchment, fill the stomach cavity with chopped onions, celery, and parsley. Squeeze lemon juice over the outside, and sprinkle all over with pickling spices. Then wrap it snugly in parchment, 3 or 4 layers of newspaper, and three gunny sacks. Fold the burlap neatly and wire in place with light wire.

Turn the hose on the package until the burlap and newspapers are soaked through. Place the bundle in a chicken wire sling and lower it into the pit on top of the coals. Cover with a piece of sheet metal, and shovel a foot of dirt on top of the covering. Build a small fire on the dirt, and keep it burning until 1 hour before removing the fish. Cook 6 hours.

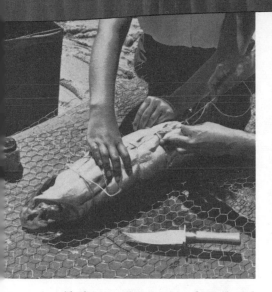

To keep stuffing in place, hold the fish together tightly, slip twine around the fish every 3 inches; tie. Push back any stuffing which comes out through head opening. Salt the outside of the fish

3

Wrap prepared fish in seaweed; place on chicken wire frame covered first with seaweed. Remove coals from pit; quickly lower frame into pit, toss vegetables, corn last, on top of wrapped fish

4

5

Cover with additional seaweed to give more flavor, moisture during cooking. Place 2 sacks over pit, tucking in the edges to keep sand from sifting through unto food. Cover with 2 inches of sand

6

Mark rim of circle clearly. Return coals to filled pit, rebuild fire, and burn 4 hours. At dinner time, scrape off fire, remove vegetables and place in separate pans; lift fish out by the wire frame

1 To cook two 130-pound pigs, dig a pit 6 feet in diameter, 18 inches deep. Let oak fire burn 2½ hours; volcanic rocks laid over oak will settle to ground level

2 Wet ti leaves, tied in bundles of 10 to 15, are thrown over rocks in pit. Pigs, in chicken wire frame, are lowered onto leaves, covered with more wet leaves

Tuna Luau

1	long fin tuna, about 25 pounds	1	cup sugar
12	large banana leaves. If not available, four clean wet gunny sacks	1	bottle Worcestershire
		½	cup prepared mustard
		2	bottles catsup

Sauce:

2	big bulbs of garlic, ground in food chopper	½	pint vinegar
½	bottle Tabasco	1	quart olive oil
		½	gallon sauterne
			Salt and pepper

Build fire in 2½-foot-deep, stone-lined pit and keep burning for at least 10 hours.

Do not clean the fish. Wrap tuna in dampened banana leaves or wet gunny sacks. Place in pit on top of hot stones, cover with ashes a foot deep, then place a layer of earth 6 inches deep over the ashes. After about 6 hours, build a fire of charcoal on top of the pit and let it burn down for about 3 hours. Combine the sauce ingredients and simmer for about 10 minutes, stirring constantly.

Now you are ready to dig out the tuna. With a shovel, place the steaming tuna on a big wooden plank, peel off the wrappings the skin, dispose of the innards. The pieces of tuna are eaten Polynesian style with the fingers, dipping the tuna into the bubbling sauce. Serve with dry white wine. Serves 15.

3 *Smashed banana stalks cover the leaves, are followed by thick coating of wet breadfruit leaves. (Corn husks or cauliflower leaves may be used instead)*

Wet gunnysacks are then stretched over heaped-up mound of leaves to protect pigs from dirt covering and to help keep the steam from escaping from pit **4**

5 *Dirt is shoveled over the sacks, starting at the outer rim first. Next step is to sprinkle whole mound with water to seal in the heat, steam, and flavor*

6 *Pigs this large require about 6½ hours cooking time (60-pound pigs pit-cook in 4½ hours). When cooking is completed, loosen the frame, remove rocks*

Open-Pit Barbecue

Ordinarily the meat chosen for a barbecue of this type is a small pig, lamb, or calf. Here are directions for cooking it:

Select first-class meat weighing from 35 to 50 pounds. Remove the head near the shoulders. Cut off the feet at the first joint. Saw the backbone through the middle lengthwise so that it will open out flat, but do not cut the carcass in halves. For lamb and veal cut off the thin flanks with a circular cut.

Run sharpened iron rods or oak sticks lengthwise through the hams and shoulders just under the skin and under the ribs. This will permit the thick parts to come nearer to the fire for better cooking and, if the rods are run through in such a way as to support them, the ribs will not fall out when the meat is tender. These rods should be long enough to rest on the banks of the pit, and also to furnish hand holds for lifting and turning. Three or four smaller rods must be stuck through the sides at intervals and held to the main rod by baling wire. This prevents the tender cooked meat from falling off.

The pit should be 16 inches deep and as wide and long as needed to accommodate the meat. The hardwood fire should have been started several hours in advance of the cooking, to be burned down to a good bed of coals. At one end of the pit, away from the meat, or in another pit, should be an auxiliary fire from which coals can be taken to add to the cooking fire as needed.

Place the meat over the fire, meat side down, until warm. Then turn meat side up and baste, using a large swab, with a strong solution of warm salt water containing a little cayenne pepper, and turn back again. The meat is cooked with the open side down, skin side up, during the first part of the cooking.

A quart of salt will be needed for a 50-pound pig. Baste as often as the meat becomes dry, and repeat until the meat is nearly done. Then increase the heat by putting more coals under the thick sections of the meat. Then baste two or three times with plain warm water to wash the excess salt from the outside. At this point the meat should be carefully watched to prevent burning. When nearly done, baste with the barbecue sauce (recipe given below).

When done and very tender, remove some of the coals from the pit and turn skin side down to brown and crisp. While meat is browning, meat side should be basted frequently with salt water and barbecue sauce. (Remember to keep both salt water and sauce warm throughout the cooking.)

When carving to serve, put the skin pieces in one pan and the meat in another. Baste the meat with the barbecue sauce, but leave the skin pieces as they are, for basting makes them gummy instead of crisp and brittle as they should be.

Barbecue sauce:

2 pounds butter	2 tablespoons Worcestershire
2½ quarts water	1 cup vinegar
1½ tablespoons dry mustard	2 teaspoons Tabasco
¼ cup sugar	3 tablespoons black pepper
3 tablespoons salt	4 tablespoons paprika
3 tablespoons chili powder	1 onion, chopped fine
½ teaspoon cayenne	1 clove garlic, minced

Mix these ingredients and boil together gently for 30 minutes before using.

Salt Steak

Wet and pack 5 or 6 pounds of rock salt around a 2 or 3-inch steak and place in paper sack. Salt coating must be at least 1 inch thick.

Bury in deep bed of glowing coals and leave 25 to 40 minutes. Break away salt crust and slice meat.

Hamburgers in Foil

Hamburger patties, sliced potatoes, and carrot sticks can be cooked together in a foil slipcover. Don't forget the salt, pepper, monosodium glutamate, and a layer of prepared mustard on the meat. This combination will require about 15 minutes of hot coal cooking.

Salmon Barbecue

To begin with, get strictly fresh fish, and allow one pound "on the hoof" for each person to be served. Silver, Spring, and Sockeye are the best varieties for the purpose. If the weather is warm, pack fish in ice until ready for use.

Start the fire four hours before serving time, on level ground. Choose a cleared spot away from any inflammable material. The fire should be long and narrow—1 foot wide and 3 feet long for the first one or two fish, then an additional 3 feet in length for every two more fish thereafter. Start it with anything handy, but feed it with half-dry alder poles. If no alder is available, use any hardwood, such as vine maple or maple. In cooking, a slow steady fire should be maintained.

Frames against which the fish are supported during the process of barbecuing are built by placing a rail the length of the fire (on both sides if more than a single salmon is to be barbecued) supported by stakes at each end. This rail should be about 2 feet from the fire and 18 inches above the ground.

Using a sharp knife, with plenty of water at hand, scale and clean the salmon in the usual manner. Then cut out the backbone by making an incision down each side of it on the inside (flesh

side), being careful not to cut through the skin. After the backbone has been removed, the fish can be flattened out, flesh side up. It is in this position that two long wooden skewers, ½ inch in diameter, are thrust entirely through the body of the fish from side to side, about 12 inches apart. These should be long enough to project about 10 inches on either side. Then salt should be rubbed generously into the fleshy side of the fish.

Next, the salted and skewered fish are stood against the rails, supported by the ends of the skewers, in a slightly slanting position. The flesh side must be toward the bed of coals. The cooking now takes about 2½ to 3 hours, and all the cook can do is watch and keep the slow, even bed of coals going.

When the fish are thoroughly done, turn each one around so that the skin side is toward the fire and allow it to cook that way for a half hour longer. This adds much to the flavor by driving the oils, which have collected in the skin, back into the meat to keep it from being dry.

Plank-Cooked Salmon

To hold an 8-pound salmon, choose a board about 18 inches wide, 36 inches long, and ¾ inch thick. Other equipment you need includes: about 2 dozen small nails, 6 yards of lightweight wire, tin scissors, and a stake about 5 feet long.

Clean and scale fish; remove head, tail, fins. Working from inside of fish, split down middle so it lies flat but is still in one piece. Cut bones away from meat. Alternate method for uncleaned fish (round): Cut off head; cut along back and slide knife down backbone and along rib bones, folding meat to one side, keeping belly side intact. Repeat on other side. Slip fish into plastic bag containing the following marinade, and let stand in cool place for at least 1 hour before cooking.

Marinade:

1 cup lemon juice	2 teaspoons dry mustard
1½ teaspoons salt	¼ cup (4 tablespoons) grated
¼ teaspoon pepper	onion
3 tablespoons brown sugar	½ cup salad oil

Combine lemon juice with salt, pepper, brown sugar, mustard, and

Secure salmon fillets with cross sticks held between paired poles. Plant poles near fire for smoke, heat. Baste often

Baste the planked salmon several times during cooking with a marinade sauce for flavor and moisture. (Recipe above)

grated onion. Stir in salad oil and beat until blended. Use both as marinade and basting sauce. Makes 1⅔ cups.

Build fire in front of rock or hill, which will reflect the heat. Mount salmon as follows: Cover one side of plank with heavy aluminum foil. Drive nail part way into each end of plank. Slide marinated fish out of bag; center on plank, skin side down. Lay 2 strips of bacon—overlapped slightly in center—across fish in 5 places. With nails, tack bacon at center and edges of fish. Cut 5 lengths of wire, wrap each piece around board at place where bacon covers fish; twist ends together. Fasten stake to nail at end of plank.

With stake for a prop, stand plank at about 75° angle in front of hot fire. Slip sheet of aluminum foil under bottom of plank and crimp edges upward to catch juices and keep sand off plank. Cook fish 30 minutes, basting occasionally. Unfasten plank from stake, turn plank upside down, put back in place to cook 30 minutes longer, or until meat flakes with fork. Serves 12 to 14.

Chuck Roast

3 pounds chuck roast, cut
 3 inches thick
1 clove garlic
¼ cup olive oil

½ jar prepared mustard
 (approximately)
Salt

Put the meat in a flat pan or on a platter. Rub it thoroughly with garlic, then smear it with olive oil. Spread plenty of mustard on it, and pat in all the salt that will cling to it. Repeat on the other side. Let stand an hour or more.

Let your fire burn down until you have a deep bed of glowing coals. Gently place the meat right on the coals—no grill. Turn only once during cooking, and allow 20 minutes to a side for rare. To serve, slice the meat in strips. Serves 4 generously.

(NOTE: The oil and mustard absorb a considerable amount of salt, thus forming a coating which adheres to the meat. This salty crust prevents the meat from becoming charred and, in addition, keeps the juices inside.)

Steak on Foil

Steak is broiled on foil, not in it. Arrange the steak on a sheet of foil, but do not wrap. Place directly on top of the hot coals and broil, turning once. The length of time required for broiling depends on whether you like rare or well-done steak.

Mollusks—Roasted

Clean and scrub shells thoroughly and place on coals. Serve with butter, salt, and pepper.

Baked Trout

1 12-inch trout	1 thin strip bacon
1/4 teaspoon salt	Maple or other sweet leaves
1/4 small onion, diced fine	

Prepare 1 trout for each person to be served.

Clean trout and cut off the head and tail. Sprinkle the salt and onion evenly inside the trout, then place the strip of bacon over the diced onion so that it will not fall out. The trout so dressed is then ready to be wrapped firmly with wet leaves, so that the entire surface is covered. The leaves will prevent the fish from sticking to the mud, and will prevent any loss of moisture from the meat.

Make a mold of wet earth or clay 2 inches thick over the side and ends of the fish, patting the mud down solidly so that the fire can reach no portion of the meat. This mud must be wet enough to mold but not so wet that it will lose shape.

After the fish is prepared in this manner, bury it in the red-hot coals of the campfire. The fire should be raked back over the fish and kept burning slowly for one hour.

Then take the fish from the fire and break open the mud shell. The skin of the trout will stick to the leaves. The fish should then be split open and the backbone removed, and the trout is ready to be served.

Foil-Wrapped Fruits and Vegetables

To cook fruits or vegetables in ashes, first wrap them securely in a double layer of foil, then place in or around the ashes. Turn once or twice during the cooking. Using a long-pronged fork, test for doneness by piercing through the foil.

Fruits

Roasted Apples. Core apples and fill holes with sugar and a piece of butter, also cinnamon or nutmeg, if desired. Wrap in foil and cook for 30 minutes, or until fork tender.

Roasted Bananas. Wrap unpeeled bananas in foil and roast like apples. Or peel, dip in melted butter, and sprinkle with sugar before wrapping.

Vegetables

Roasted Beets. Wrap whole unpeeled beets in foil and roast until tender. Serve with butter and lemon wedges, and let guests peel and season their own beets. Or peel beets before roasting and wrap in foil.

Roasted Corn. Husk corn, brush with butter, and wrap in foil before roasting. Turn occasionally during the cooking. Corn will take 10 or 15 minutes. Another method of roasting corn is in the husks: Peel back husks, remove silk with a brush, replace husks, and wire or tie ends. Soak in cold water for half an hour before roasting in or around the ashes.

Roasted Eggplant. Wrap a whole eggplant in foil and roast it over the coals, placing it on the spit if desired. When fork tender, the skin will peel off easily. Eggplant may also be roasted on a spit without the foil wrapping.

Roasted Onions. Wrap whole peeled or unpeeled onions in foil, and roast until fork tender. Serve with butter.

Roasted Potatoes. Wrap unpeeled potatoes in foil and roast as you would onions. Or, if you like a hard, blackened skin—and many do—roast potatoes without wrapping. Cook potatoes until fork tender, and turn during the cooking. They will take from 30 to 60 minutes. Serve with plenty of butter, or with sour cream and chives.

Roasted Sweet Potatoes or Yams. Cook exactly as directed for white potatoes.

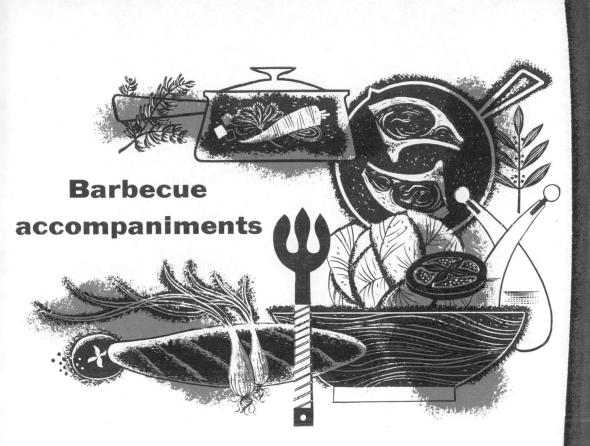

Barbecue accompaniments

The *pièce de résistance* of your barbecue meal will, of course, be the meat, fowl, or fish that you lift piping hot from the grill, the spit, or the coals. Generally your guests will have watched with growing appetites as this main dish sizzled away on the barbecue. The side dishes that you serve with this flavorsome main course should not in any way detract from it; yet they should be sufficient to satisfy the hearty appetites that go with outdoor dining.

Principal things to consider in planning your menu are (1) that the accompaniments can be prepared ahead of time or can be cooked right on the barbecue, and (2) that they will hold up well while the main course is being cooked and served. Your choice might include a casserole that can be prepared in the kitchen before your guests arrive and can be kept warm at the edge of the fire. Most barbecue menus include a salad. This, too, can be prepared in advance; the dressing can be added at the last minute.

Mexican foods are good complements to barbecued meats, and Mexican theme is carried out here in gay table setting.

Food is served in sturdy pottery dishes, Mexican baskets. Striped awning, travel posters add to south-of-border feeling

Cold vegetable dishes, relishes, and fruit platters are good choices. There are many skillet dishes that you can cook right on the grill and, like the casserole, they can be kept warm near the fire until serving time.

The recipes included in this chapter were selected primarily because of the ease with which they can be prepared and served. Whatever your choice of accompaniments may be, remember to keep them simple so that you, too, can enjoy the barbecuing of the main course.

CASSEROLES

If you plan to serve a casserole, select one that is light and not too filling so that there will be no chance of its competing with the main course. If you are serving barbecued meat, you will probably want to select a casserole that does not have meat as one of its

Hearts of palm are a menu surprise on barbecue table. Cut canned palm pieces in half lengthwise; pour over them red table wine, olive oil. Top with ground pepper, pimiento. Chill a few hours

Stuff pimientos with mixture of 3 eggs (beaten), 2 cups cooked corn, 1 tablespoon melted butter, salt and pepper. Arrange in casserole; bake uncovered at 350° for 20 minutes or until firm

To make sesame bread, cut French bread in ½-inch slices, brush one side with melted butter, dip buttered side in toasted sesame seeds. Place on cooky sheet and toast lightly under broiler

For colorful Thousand Island dressing, add chopped beets, chopped green pepper, sliced celery, chopped egg to your favorite recipe. Arrange lettuce wedges on plate and spoon dressing over them

principal ingredients. Most of the recipes that follow are pastes or vegetable combinations that are fitting accompaniments to barbecued meats and yet do not overpower them.

Noodles Romanoff

In this ideal accompaniment for barbecued meat, the sour cream really asserts itself and gives the noodles character.

1 package (8 oz.) egg noodles	1 cup (½ pint) thick cultured sour cream
1 cup large curd cottage cheese	¼ cup grated onion
1 small clove garlic, minced or mashed	¼ teaspoon Tabasco
1 teaspoon Worcestershire	½ cup grated processed Cheddar cheese

Cook the noodles until just tender in boiling salted water. Combine drained noodles, cottage cheese, garlic, Worcestershire, sour cream, grated onion, and Tabasco. If you like a very colorful casserole, add some chopped pimiento or green pepper. Turn into a buttered casserole; sprinkle grated cheese over the top. Bake in a moderate oven (350°) for 25 minutes, or until heated through. Serves 8.

Canned beans garnished with pineapple kept warm in electrically heated bean pot. If you have outlet near barbecue, you will find automatic cookers useful in keeping cooked foods at serving heat

1

Chilled, cooked, green beans are served here with tarragon sauce. To make the sauce, combine 1 cup mayonnaise with 2 tablespoons of prepared mustard and ½ teaspoon crumbled, dried tarragon

2

Red onions complement the beans and mushrooms in color and flavor. Slice them paper thin, soak in ice water, and drain. Dress onions with a little wine vinegar, season with salt and pepper

3

Prepare mushroom caps the night before barbecue. Poach 2 pounds of caps for 6 minutes in 1 cup dry white table wine, 2 tablespoons oil, 1 tablespoon dried tarragon. Refrigerate overnight

Noodles Alfredo

1 pound narrow noodles or fettucini	1/3 cup grated Parmesan cheese
1/2 cup (1 cube) butter	1/3 cup grated Swiss cheese
	1/2 cup hot heavy cream

Cook the noodles in boiling salted water until barely tender. Drain and dress immediately with the butter, which has been melted and is still very hot, and the Parmesan and Swiss cheeses. Mix with a fork and spoon, lifting the noodles high so that the steam will escape. When each noodle is well coated with cheese place in casserole, pour heated cream over the noodles, mix lightly, and serve at once. Serves 6.

Oriental Green Rice

3 tablespoons butter	1 teaspoon salt
1/8 teaspoon curry powder	1/4 cup finely chopped peanuts or toasted almonds
3 cups cooked rice	
1/3 cup finely chopped parsley	

Melt butter, add curry powder, and blend. Combine with rice. Season with parsley, salt, and chopped peanuts. Place in casserole or baking pan. Heat 15 to 20 minutes before serving. Serves 6.

Macaroni and Cheese

1 1/2 cups elbow macaroni, uncooked	1 1/2 tablespoons pimiento, chopped fine
1/4 cup butter	1 teaspoon salt
1 1/2 cups American cheese, cubed	1/8 teaspoon pepper
1 1/2 tablespoons onion, chopped	1/2 teaspoon paprika
1 1/2 tablespoons parsley, chopped fine	2 eggs
	2 cups milk

Cook the macaroni in boiling salted water for 15 minutes. Drain and pour cold water through it. Put it in a buttered baking dish. Add the butter, cubed cheese, chopped onion, parsley, pimiento and seasonings to the macaroni. Beat the eggs slightly and add milk to them. Pour over the macaroni and cheese and bake, uncovered, at 325° for 50 minutes. Serves 6.

Macaroni Bake

2 cups shell macaroni	2 tablespoons Worcestershire
1 cup cottage cheese	1 tablespoon chili sauce
1 cup sour cream	2 drops Tabasco
1 clove garlic, minced	Salt and pepper to taste
1 medium sized onion, minced	Grated Parmesan cheese

Cook macaroni in boiling salted water until just tender. Drain, and rinse with cold water. Place in bowl and combine with cottage cheese, sour cream, garlic, onion, Worcestershire, chili sauce, Tabasco, salt and pepper. Turn into a greased casserole and bake at 350° for about 45 minutes. Sprinkle with cheese, then return to the oven for a few minutes before serving. Serves 6.

Green Pepper-Cheese Casserole

Butter or margarine	2 cups chopped or grated
6 large green peppers	Cheddar cheese
3 cups cooked rice	Salt and pepper to taste

Grease an 8 to 10-inch baking casserole with butter or margarine. Cut green peppers in half, remove seeds, rinse, and steam until tender. Put a layer of rice in the bottom of the casserole, then a layer of steamed green pepper, then a layer of cheese, and so on. If the rice seems dry, as day-old cooked rice sometimes does, dot the rice layers with butter. Finish off with a layer of cheese. Place in oven, preheated to 350° (moderate), and bake 30 to 40 minutes. Serves 6.

Squash With Almonds

1 pound yellow crookneck squash	1/8 teaspoon ginger
1/4 cup butter	1/4 cup brown sugar
Salt and pepper to taste	1/2 cup finely sliced almonds
1/4 teaspoon basil	(or as many as the budget will allow)
1/2 cup heavy cream	

Split squash. In frying pan melt butter, add squash, and brown lightly. Sprinkle with salt, pepper, and basil. Put all in casserole, add cream, dust with ginger, sprinkle on brown sugar, and top with sliced almonds. Bake at 350° for about 20 minutes, or until tender and the top is brown. Serves 4 to 6.

Baked Zucchini Casserole

2 pounds zucchini	2 tablespoons minced parsley
½ teaspoon salt	1 cup (¼ lb.) grated
2 medium sized onions, minced	Cheddar cheese
1 clove garlic, minced or mashed	4 eggs
	½ teaspoon Worcestershire
1 tablespoon butter or margarine	Dash of Tabasco
	1 teaspoon salt
3 slices fresh bread, cut in small cubes	½ teaspoon each pepper and paprika

Remove ends of zucchini, and cook in a small amount of water with the ½ teaspoon of salt until tender. Drain and mash zucchini to medium smoothness. Sauté onion and garlic in the butter, and add to zucchini along with cubed bread, minced parsley, cheese, well-beaten eggs, and seasonings. Mix well and spoon into a well-buttered baking dish. Set in a pan of hot water and bake in a moderate oven (350°) for 30 minutes, or until firm. Serves 6 to 8.

Green Beans Supreme

The simplicity of this dish, made from three canned items in your larder, makes it suitable for spur-of-the-moment entertaining.

1 can (No. 303) green beans, drained	¼ teaspoon oregano (optional)
	1 can (3½ oz.) French fried onions
1 can (10½ oz.) mushroom soup	

Mix the green beans, undiluted mushroom soup, and oregano in a 9-inch square or round baking dish. Bake in a moderate oven (350°) for 15 minutes. Sprinkle with French fried onions, and continue baking for 5 more minutes. Serves 4 generously.

You may substitute 2 packages of partially cooked frozen green beans for the canned ones.

Smoky Beans

For quick baked beans, season canned baked beans with a small amount of liquid smoke, then place in a bean pot with a good-sized onion buried in the center. Strip bacon across the top. Bake in a moderately hot oven (375°) for about 45 minutes.

Three-Bean Casserole

1 large onion, finely chopped
1 clove garlic, mashed or minced
3 tablespoons bacon drippings
2 packages (10 oz. each) frozen lima beans
1 can (No. 300) tomato style baked beans

1 can (No. 303) red kidney beans
1/2 cup catsup
1/4 cup (4 tablespoons) water
3 tablespoons vinegar
1 tablespoon brown sugar
1 teaspoon dry mustard
1 teaspoon salt
1/4 teaspoon pepper

In a large, heavy frying pan, sauté onion and garlic in bacon drippings until golden brown. While onion is cooking, cook limas in boiling salted water 16 to 18 minutes, or until tender; drain and add to sautéed onion, along with baked beans, kidney beans, catsup, water, vinegar, brown sugar, mustard, salt, and pepper. Heat mixture, then turn into a 2-quart casserole. Bake in a moderate oven (350°) for 30 minutes. Serves 6 to 8.

Onion Sour Cream Pie

The sautéed onions in this custard-like pie surprise you with their sweet flavor.

2 1/2 pounds onions
3 tablespoons butter or margarine
1 cup (1/2 pint) thick commercial sour cream
3 eggs
1/4 cup (4 tablespoons) sherry
1/4 teaspoon salt

Dash of pepper
1/8 teaspoon each nutmeg, thyme, mace, and powdered cloves
10-inch unbaked pastry shell
1 strip of bacon, cut in small pieces
Paprika

Peel onions, slice thinly, and sauté in melted butter until golden brown. Cool thoroughly; then stir in sour cream. Beat eggs well, then stir in wine, salt, pepper, nutmeg, thyme, mace, and cloves. Combine the sautéed onions and sour cream with the egg mixture and turn into the pastry shell. Sprinkle bacon over the top. Bake in a moderate oven (350°) for 1 hour, or until the custard is set. Sprinkle with paprika; cut in wedges. Serves 8.

Baked Onions With Almonds

Onions, either raw or cooked, are well suited to barbecue menus. This onion dish goes well with any type of meat. Almonds are an excellent texture contrast. Or you can substitute filberts as the nut meats.

6 large onions	1/2 teaspoon salt
1/2 teaspoon salt	1/4 teaspoon freshly ground
1 can (10 1/2 oz.) cream of	pepper
mushroom soup	1/4 teaspoon paprika
1 cup milk	2 cups chopped almond meats

Peel onions, quarter, and cook in a small amount of boiling water with the 1/2 teaspoon salt until almost tender; drain. Mix together mushroom soup, milk, 1/2 teaspoon salt, pepper, and paprika; pour over the cooked onions. Turn half of the onions and sauce into a round, 9-inch casserole and sprinkle with 1 cup of nut meats; cover with the remaining onions and sprinkle the top with the remaining cup of nut meats. Bake in a hot oven (400°) for 20 minutes, then place under the boiler to brown the top lightly (about 2 minutes). Serves 6 generously.

Corn Pudding

This corn pudding made with freshly grated corn and cornmeal is similar to a meatless tamale pie. Because this dish takes the place of both vegetable and rice or potatoes, it needs only an accompaniment of meat from the barbecue.

2 eggs	1 cup pitted ripe olives
1 1/4 cups milk	1 teaspoon salt
2 1/2 cups grated raw corn	1/4 teaspoon each pepper,
1 cup chopped tomatoes	paprika, and chili powder
1 small onion, finely chopped	1 cup yellow cornmeal
1 green pepper, seeded and	1/2 cup (1 cube) butter or
chopped	margarine
1 can (4 oz.) pimientos,	
chopped	

Beat eggs slightly; stir in milk, corn, tomatoes, onion, green pepper, pimientos, olives, salt, pepper, paprika, and chili powder. Add cornmeal, and stir until well mixed. Melt butter; stir into cornmeal mixture. Turn into a greased 2-quart casserole. Bake in a moderately slow oven (325°) for 1 hour, or until firm. Serves 6.

Cheese and Hominy Casserole

Chopped green chili peppers add a desirable spiciness to the ground hominy in this casserole.

3 medium sized onions
2 cans (No. 303 each) hominy
2 cans (4 oz. each) green chili peppers

1 clove garlic, minced or mashed
4 cups (1 lb.) grated Cheddar cheese

Put onions and hominy through food chopper, using medium blade, and mix together. Remove seeds and chop chili peppers; mix with garlic. In a greased 9-inch round casserole, arrange alternate layers of the hominy and onions, chili peppers and garlic, and cheese, ending with the cheese. Bake in a moderate oven (350°) for 45 minutes. Serves 6 to 8.

Ranchers' Spoon Bread

The Italian cook discovered long ago that cooked ground corn is an excellent accompaniment to chicken. Use either regular corn-meal or coarsely ground Italian-style *polenta* in this recipe.

2¼ cups milk
¾ cup yellow cornmeal or polenta
¼ cup sugar

½ teaspoon salt
½ cup (1 cube) butter or margarine
3 eggs, separated

Heat milk just to boiling; stirring constantly, add cornmeal gradually and cook until cornmeal begins to thicken. Add sugar and salt, and stirring occasionally, cook until cornmeal is thick. Remove from heat and stir in butter. Beat egg yolks slightly; stir in a little of the cornmeal mixture. Add the egg yolks to hot corn-meal and mix well. Beat egg whites until stiff; fold into cornmeal mixture.

Turn into a greased 1½-quart casserole. Bake in a moderately hot oven (375°) for 35 minutes, or until a knife inserted in the center comes out clean. Serve with butter or gravy. Serves 6.

Mashed Potato-Ripe Olive Casserole

Mash potatoes as usual; season with salt, pepper, and butter; stud with plenty of sliced ripe olives. Pile mixture lightly in a buttered casserole, and reheat and brown in the kitchen oven before serving.

Curried Lima Casserole

2 packages (10 oz. each) frozen baby lima beans	1 cup chili sauce
1 can (10½ oz.) cream of mushroom soup	2 tablespoons maple syrup
	2 teaspoons curry powder
	2 tablespoons brown sugar

Cook the lima beans 10 minutes in 1 cup unsalted water. Stir in all the above ingredients and pour into casserole. Bake uncovered for 30 minutes at 350°. Serves 6.

SKILLET FARE

Many barbecue chefs have learned that it is a simple matter to cook a rice or vegetable dish right on the grill while the meat is barbecuing. Advance preparations can be done in the kitchen, and the dish can then be set over low coals to bubble away until serving time.

Barbecue Style Peas

Here is a method of serving tender young peas that we think will go over well at your next barbecue.

2 pounds fresh green peas	½ teaspoon sugar
½ cup boiling water	½ cup (1 cube) melted butter or margarine
½ teaspoon salt	

Wash pea pods thoroughly, then place in a saucepan with the water, salt, and sugar. Cover and cook on the grill just until peas are tender, about 10 minutes. (Peas cook in the pod more quickly than when shelled. If overcooked, the pods will open.) Divide the melted butter among 6 tall cordial glasses, or any small slender glasses available. Heat glasses or stand them in hot water until ready to use so that the butter will remain melted.

Pass the cooked unshelled peas in a large bowl, or serve in individual bowls. You dip the pods into the melted butter and then suck the peas into your mouth, much as you eat cocktail tamales. Provide a basket or some container for the discarded pods. Serves 6.

Chili Fandango

2 bell peppers
1/4 pound sliced bacon, diced
1 onion, minced
1 clove garlic, minced

4 large tomatoes, peeled and diced
1/4 teaspoon salt

Toast bell peppers over coals until black. Scrape off black skins, and cut each pepper into 3 or 4 pieces. Fry bacon, onion, and garlic together until crisp and brown. Add peppers, tomatoes, and salt. Cook slowly in covered pan for 35 minutes. Serves 6.

Mexican Beans

2 cups pinto beans
1 1/2 cloves garlic
2 medium onions, chopped
3 green peppers

2 teaspoons salt
1/2 teaspoon black pepper
1 tablespoon bacon fat

Wash beans; place in a heavy kettle with water; cover, bring to a boil, and simmer 2 minutes. Remove from heat and let soak 1 hour.

Put fat in skillet; add chopped onion, garlic, peppers, salt and pepper; let cook 5 minutes; then add to beans in pot with enough water to cover. Let boil slowly until thoroughly soft, but not mushy. Add hot water if necessary during the cooking. Warm up or finish cooking on the grill. Serves 6.

Corn Chowder

Steaming corn chowder can be cooked quickly and easily in a skillet over your barbecue grill. Here's how:

4 slices bacon
2 medium sized onions
3 medium sized potatoes
3 cups water

1 teaspoon salt
2 cans (No. 303) corn
1 can tomato soup
1 small can evaporated milk

Cut bacon into small pieces and brown; add finely chopped onions. Return to grill and brown slightly. To this mixture, add sliced potatoes, water, and salt. Cook until potato bits are tender; then add corn and tomato soup. Boil for a few minutes and add milk. If you like, you may add cubes of ham and cook a few more minutes. Serves 3 or 4.

Cowboy Corn

1/4 pound bacon or salt pork, diced	1 green pepper, finely chopped
2 cans (No. 303) whole kernel corn	Onion, celery, garlic, chili powder, and pepper to taste

Fry the bacon or salt pork lightly. Drain the juice from the canned corn and save this liquor to use later. Dump the corn into the hot skillet and let it sizzle for two or three minutes before stirring. Drop into this the green pepper (or red pepper if you want it hot) and other seasonings.

When everything is mixed thoroughly, empty the corn liquor into the pan. If this doesn't furnish enough moisture, add fresh or evaporated milk. Let it simmer, with a top on the pan, until liquid substances have almost disappeared. With tortillas replacing silverware, you'll have a real taste treat. Serves 6.

Sautéed Corn

6 medium sized ears corn	1/4 cup (4 tablespoons) table cream
3 tablespoons butter or margarine	Salt and pepper

Cut raw corn from the cob. Melt butter in a heavy frying pan; add corn, and stirring constantly, sauté until it begins to brown. Add cream and salt and pepper to taste. Heat thoroughly but do not allow to boil. Serves 4.

Hominy Rio Grande

1 onion, minced	1 teaspoon sugar
2 tablespoons salad oil	1 cup uncooked hominy grits (cook ahead of time in salted water) or 1 large can (No. 2 1/2) hominy
1 pound fresh tomatoes, chopped, or 1 can (No. 2) solid pack tomatoes	
1/4 teaspoon chili powder	1 cup grated sharp cheese
1 teaspoon salt	

Brown onion lightly in oil. Add tomatoes, chili powder, salt, and sugar. Cover and cook slowly on top of barbecue until most of liquid has cooked down. Add cooked hominy grits. Mix in cheese and stir until melted. Remove from heat and serve at once. Serves 4 to 6.

Potato Pancakes

6 medium sized raw potatoes	1 tablespoon milk
1 onion	1 teaspoon salt
2 eggs, beaten	Pepper
2 tablespoons flour	Oil or bacon drippings

Grate the potatoes and onion; mix in the eggs, flour, milk, salt, and pepper, and add a little oil or bacon drippings. Shape into flat cakes 2 or 3 inches across, and pan-fry to a golden brown. Serves 6.

Colache

1 pound summer squash	1 small onion, finely chopped
4 ears of corn	1/4 cup butter
3 tomatoes	Salt and pepper

Dice or slice squash; cut corn off cob (or use canned); peel and dice tomatoes (or use canned). Sauté onion in butter, add vegetables. Season to taste. Cover, and cook outside at barbecue for 30 to 35 minutes, while meat is cooking. Stir occasionally so vegetables won't burn. Serves 6.

Garden Bouquet

1 can (No. 2 1/2) tomatoes	1 tablespoon sugar
1 tablespoon butter	1 cup celery
Salt and pepper to taste	3 tablespoons parsley (packed)

Heat tomatoes steaming hot, not boiling. Add butter, salt, pepper, and sugar. Last, add the celery, chopped fine, and chopped parsley. Serve at once. Serves 4.

Tomatoes and Peppers

Wash bell peppers (allow 2 or 3 per person) and soak in ice water for an hour; then dice in about inch squares, discarding the coarse membrane and seeds. Cook in several tablespoons of hot olive oil until soft and slightly browned. Pour off all excess oil and add as much peeled and chopped tomatoes as there are peppers. Season with salt and pepper. Push to back of grill and cook slowly for 20 to 30 minutes. Serve as a side dish with barbecued meats.

Sautéed Carrots Chateau

1 tablespoon butter or other
   shortening
2 cups carrots, diced and
   cooked until tender

1½ cups California Tokay or
   Angelica
2 tablespoons lemon juice
Salt and pepper to taste

Melt butter in frying pan and allow carrots to sauté slowly until slightly browned. Combine wine and lemon juice and pour over carrots. Simmer slowly until candied, and season to taste. Serves 4.

Golden Toasted Rice

1 cup uncooked rice
2 tablespoons butter or
   margarine
1 can (11 oz.) consommé

½ cup water
3 or 4 green onions
1 to 3 tablespoons soy

Toast the rice by spreading the grains in a heavy pan and heating in a moderate oven (350°) until lightly browned.

Melt butter in a heavy pan with a tight fitting cover; add rice and cook it slightly, stirring constantly. Pour in hot consommé and water, stir once, cover, and turn heat to the lowest possible point. Let rice steam for 25 minutes.

Stir in finely sliced green onions and tops and the soy. Remove from heat, put on the cover again, and let stand a few minutes to blend the flavors and partially cook the onion. Serves 4.

Risotto a la Ratto

1 small yellow onion, chopped
2 tablespoons butter or
   margarine
1 cup uncooked white rice
4 cups clear chicken broth

1 can (4 oz.) button mushrooms
Salt to taste
½ teaspoon saffron
½ cup grated Parmesan-type
   cheese

Sauté onion in butter until transparent but not brown. Add rice and stir until each grain is coated with the butter. Add 1 cup boiling chicken broth and cook, uncovered, over low fire, stirring frequently, until rice has absorbed liquid. Repeat process with remaining broth, adding 1 cup at a time as rice absorbs it. (This will take about 20 minutes.) Add mushrooms and salt, then stir in saffron which has been dissolved in 1 tablespoon hot water or broth. Cook 5 minutes longer. Blend in the grated cheese, and serve at once. Serves 4.

Pilaff

Pilaff makes an excellent rice accompaniment for shish kebabs and may be eaten with or without the sauce. If you wish, you can use regular or quick-cooking cracked wheat instead of rice. Many people feel that rice is best with fowl and wheat with meats, but there is no rule.

Broth for pilaff

For 6 to 8 persons make 1 quart of broth. Cover with water the lamb bones and trimmings left over after making shish kebab. Season with vegetables and herbs. After the broth cooks down, strain before using in the pilaff.

Preparation of pilaff

2 cups uncooked rice or cracked wheat (do not wash)	1 cup uncooked fine noodles 4 tablespoons butter (½ cube) 4 cups boiling broth

Use long-grained white rice. Buy barley noodles from an Armenian or Italian store. If you can't get them, use the thinnest egg noodles obtainable and crush them until they are all broken into small pieces about ½ inch long or less.

Brown the noodles in the butter until tan, pour in the rice, and mix well. The rice should not fry but should merely become covered with the butter. Pour over it the boiling broth, cover, and allow to simmer slowly without stirring for 20 minutes or until all broth has simmered away. It can be reheated by adding a little water and steaming for a short time. Serves 6 to 8.

Brown Rice Pilaff

Fry 1 cup of uncooked brown rice in 3 tablespoons of oil in a large skillet. Stir it constantly until it turns a golden brown. Then season it and pour on enough soup stock or canned bouillon to cover. (This should take slightly more than 2 cups.) Cover the pan and simmer over a slow fire until all the liquid is absorbed and the rice is almost dry. Then top it with butter and serve. Serves 4.

SALADS

The best possible complement to barbecued meat is a crisp, cool salad, skillfully torn and tossed, deftly seasoned. The dressing may be varied by the addition of such seasonings as toasted sesame seeds, anchovy paste, or minced herbs. Fruits and vegetables, either raw or cooked, may be tossed into the salad to add color and texture. The list is endless—tomatoes, sweet onion, green pepper, radishes, diced avocado, and cucumbers are some of the most common additions. Some more unusual ones you may wish to try are raw or slightly cooked asparagus tips, sliced raw or cooked mushrooms, artichoke hearts, grated raw beets, hearts of palm, seedless grapes, or sliced apple.

French Dressing

¾ cup salad oil or olive oil
1 clove garlic, sliced
    lengthwise
¼ cup vinegar or lemon juice
1 teaspoon sugar

½ teaspoon salt
Freshly ground pepper
Paprika

Measure oil into fruit jar; add garlic and let stand for several hours. Remove garlic if only mild flavor is desired. Add remainder of ingredients, cover jar tightly and shake contents until well blended. Chill before using. Makes 1 cup dressing.

Cabbage Salad a la Miller

6 firm cabbages, shredded
6 medium onions, shredded
16 carrots (approximately),
    shredded
1 teaspoon celery seed

1 jar (8 oz.) sweet pickle relish
French dressing
Mayonnaise
Salt and garlic salt to taste

Mix vegetables, celery seed, and relish thoroughly, and marinate in French dressing for about 30 minutes. Drain and add mayonnaise to your liking, then season with salt and garlic salt to taste. Arrange in large bowl and garnish with chopped ripe olives, parsley, and paprika. Serves 30.

Caesar Salad

1 large clove garlic
4 small heads romaine
2 eggs, boiled 1 minute
¾ cup grated Parmesan cheese
1 teaspoon Worcestershire
¼ cup olive oil

2 tablespoons tarragon wine
   vinegar
2 cups croutons, made from
   sour French bread
Salt and freshly ground
   pepper
Juice of 1 lemon

Mash garlic clove in salad bowl and rub around sides. Add romaine, torn in fairly large pieces. Mix in olive oil until each leaf is coated. Scoop the soft cooked eggs out onto the greens. Add other ingredients, using lemon juice last. Toss well.

Barbecue-Salad Dressing

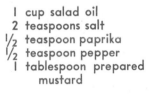

1 cup salad oil
2 teaspoons salt
½ teaspoon paprika
½ teaspoon pepper
1 tablespoon prepared
   mustard

3 drops Worcestershire
¼ cup tarragon vinegar
¼ cup cider vinegar
2 cloves garlic, cut in half

Mix thoroughly with a rotary beater. After allowing the garlic to impart its flavor, remove it.

About 30 minutes before broiling lamb chops or steaks, brush the meat liberally with some of this dressing. Then dip a swab of celery leaves in the dressing and baste the meat with it while cooking.

To what is left of the dressing, add ½ cup oil, and a dash of sugar, if desired, and stir vigorously. Pour it over crisp mixed greens for a simple tossed salad.

Dressing for Tossed Salad

1 medium sized onion, grated
3 cloves garlic, grated
1 tablespoon each salt, sugar,
   dry mustard, and crushed
   dry tarragon

½ teaspoon freshly ground
   black pepper
1 cup catsup
1 cup vinegar
2 cups oil

Mix together the onion, garlic, and seasonings in a quart jar. Pour in catsup, vinegar, and oil, and shake until thoroughly blended.

Dressing in Quantity

1 can (10½ oz.) condensed
  tomato soup
10½ oz. olive oil
10½ oz. red wine vinegar

2 onions, quartered
Garlic to taste
Salt and pepper

Empty can of tomato soup into bowl, refill can with olive oil and pour into bowl, refill can again with the vinegar, and add to the tomato-oil mixture. Add quartered onions, garlic, salt, and pepper; blend ingredients. Let stand overnight and then remove onions.

Gorgonzola Dressing

¼ pound Gorgonzola cheese,
  crumbled
2 cloves garlic, chopped fine
¼ teaspoon salt
1 tablespoon wine vinegar

¼ teaspoon freshly ground
  pepper
1 tablespoon Worcestershire
4 tablespoons olive oil

Combine all ingredients, and let stand in a warm place until flavors work through, stirring occasionally. This will make enough dressing for a salad for 4.

Variation:

Mix in blender to produce thick, creamy dressing.

Fiesta Salad

1 cup mayonnaise
1 teaspoon chili powder
Dash of catsup or chili sauce
Dash of cayenne
Salt and pepper to taste
1 can (No. 303) unflavored
  red beans

1 cucumber, diced
1 small onion, finely chopped
1 bell pepper, diced
3 large tomatoes, diced
4 slices bacon, cooked
  and crumbled

Combine the mayonnaise and seasonings in a salad bowl. Add drained beans and other vegetables. Mix well and chill. Add the bacon at the last minute to retain its crispness. Garnish with lettuce before serving. Serves 6 to 8.

Green Salad With Herb Dressing

1 cup salad oil
2 cloves garlic, cut in halves
2 tablespoons minced
   green onion
2 teaspoons each chopped
   fresh basil and tarragon
1 pinch crumbled rosemary
1 teaspoon salt

1/2 teaspoon coarse black
   pepper
2 tablespoons sugar
1/2 teaspoon dry mustard
2/3 cup wine vinegar
1 large head crisp lettuce
1 head romaine
   Watercress
   Few sprigs parsley

Place salad oil into pint fruit jar. Drop cut cloves of garlic into oil and let stand for 2 or 3 hours. Remove garlic. To oil add onion, herbs, salt, pepper, sugar, and mustard. Pour vinegar in slowly, stirring well. Place cover on jar and shake to combine ingredients. Wash salad greens and tie in a damp cloth; keep cold. Just before serving, tear greens and place in a salad bowl. Toss lightly with the herb dressing. Serves 6.

Mandros Salad

1 clove garlic
1 head lettuce, torn
1 cucumber, diced
1 dill pickle, diced
1 large carrot, diced
   Stuffed olives, sliced
1 small can anchovies
1 can asparagus, or fresh
   equivalent, cut up, and
   cooked

6 or 7 radishes, sliced
3 stalks celery, sliced
3 green onions, sliced
1 pinch each of the following
   herbs: rosemary, oregano,
   sage, basil, thyme,
   marjoram, and savory
Olive oil
Tarragon wine vinegar

Rub salad bowl with garlic. Put lettuce in first, then remaining ingredients in order listed. Dress the salad with olive oil and wine vinegar. Toss lightly. Garnishes may be hard cooked egg slices, stuffed olives, asparagus tips, cucumber rings, slivered green beans, and radish roses.

Smoky Salad Dressing

1/2 teaspoon dry mustard
   Dash of garlic oil
2 drops liquid smoke
   Pinch salt
1 teaspon soy sauce

1 tablespoon wine vinegar
1/2 teaspoon lime or lemon juice
3 tablespoons salad oil
   (delicate flavor of olive oil is
   lost in this blend)

Whip together with a fork, pour over torn lettuce, toss and serve.

Tomato and Herb Salad

Slice firm tomatoes into medium-thick slices and spread on a large platter. Anoint with a few drops of olive oil and wine vinegar, then sprinkle thickly with chopped herbs—parsley, chives, tarragon, basil, dill, and any others of your choice. Chill thoroughly. This salad can be made well in advance of the barbecue. Store in refrigerator.

Twenty-Four-Hour Fruit Salad

Here's a salad that teams up well with wild game, chicken, or grilled ham.

Juice of 3 lemons	1 can grated pineapple
Grated rind of 1½ lemons	1 pound Thompson seedless
½ cup sugar	grapes
3 egg yolks, beaten	1 cup chopped walnuts
1 pint cream	1 cup marshmallows, cut up

Cook lemon, sugar, and eggs in double boiler and cool. Whip the cream, mix with lemon custard, and work in the fruit and marshmallows. Let stand in refrigerator overnight.

Bean and Celery Salad

This hearty salad—a mixture of kidney beans, celery, and olives —is good with a barbecue dinner.

1 medium can (No. 303) kidney beans	3 tablespoons mayonnaise
2 cups sliced celery	2 tablespoons evaporated milk
1 small onion, finely chopped	1 teaspoon tarragon vinegar
2 tablespoons sliced stuffed olives	1 teaspoon sugar
½ teaspoon salt	Dash each salt, garlic salt, and paprika
Freshly ground pepper to taste	1 hard-cooked egg

Drain juice from beans and rinse them with cold water. Toss beans lightly with celery, onion, stuffed olives, salt, and pepper to taste. Chill.

When ready to serve the salad, mix together mayonnaise, milk, vinegar, sugar, salt, garlic salt, and paprika. Pour over beans, fold together, and garnish with the hard-cooked egg you have sliced or chopped. Serves 4 to 6.

Mixed Vegetable Salad

3 large bunches romaine
6 large heads lettuce
1 large bunch celery, sliced
2 packages (10 oz.) frozen
    peas, cooked and chilled

1 bunch carrots, shredded
1 bunch radishes, sliced, or
    4 tomatoes, cut in wedges
1 pint French dressing

Tear romaine and lettuce into pieces; add celery, peas, carrots, and radishes. Toss with dressing before serving. Serves 24.

Mushroom-Olive Salad

1 teaspoon salt
1 tablespoon water
1 clove garlic, minced
2/3 cup salad oil
1/4 cup vinegar
2 teaspoons lemon juice
1 teaspoon sugar
1/2 teaspoon each dry mustard,
    rosemary, and Worcester-
    shire

1 can (4 oz.) button mush-
    rooms, drained
1 medium sized head lettuce,
    torn in shreds
1/2 cup sliced celery
3 green onions and tops,
    chopped
1 tablespoon minced parsley
1/4 cup stuffed green olives,
    sliced

Dissolve salt in water; add garlic and let stand for at least 30 minutes; stir occasionally. Mix together the salad oil, vinegar, lemon juice, sugar, mustard, rosemary, Worcestershire, and drained mushrooms. Strain garlic and add garlic water to dressing. Let stand 20 minutes. Remove mushrooms and arrange with lettuce, celery, onions, parsley, and olives in a bowl; pour over dressing and toss lightly. Serves 6.

Tossed Cauliflower Salad

1 medium sized head of
    cauliflower
1/2 cup French dressing
1 small avocado
1/2 cup sliced stuffed green
    olives

3 tomatoes, cut in eighths
1/2 cup Roquefort cheese,
    crumbled
Crisp greens

Separate cauliflower into flowerets; cover with ice water and chill 1 hour; drain. Chop cauliflower coarsely; pour over French dressing and let stand 2 hours. Just before serving, dice avocado and add to salad along with olives, tomatoes, and cheese. Toss lightly; serve on crisp greens. Serves 8.

Hearty Vegetable Salad

1 small cauliflower
1/4 cup French dressing
2 cups shredded raw cabbage
1 package (10 oz.) frozen green peas or 1 1/2 cups fresh peas, cooked
1/4 pound raw spinach, shredded
1/4 cup finely minced onion
1 small carrot, grated
1 cup sliced celery
1 cup cooked frozen or fresh small green lima beans
1/4 teaspoon salt
Pepper to taste
1/2 cup each French dressing and mayonnaise
Lettuce cups
Paprika

Cook cauliflower in boiling salted water until barely tender; drain and let cool. Separate into flowerets, and marinate in the 1/4 cup French dressing, turning the cauliflowerets so they are well coated with dressing. Chill.

Toss together lightly the cabbage, peas, spinach, onion, carrot, celery, lima beans, salt, and pepper to taste. Blend together the French dressing and mayonnaise and toss with the mixed vegetables, including the cauliflowerets. Pile into a lettuce-lined bowl and sprinkle with paprika. Serves 10.

Mexican Salad Bowl

4 slices bread, cut in 1/2-inch cubes
1 tablespoon butter or margarine
1 clove of garlic, minced or mashed
1/2 cup sliced celery
1/2 cup finely sliced onion, separated into rings
1/2 green pepper, sliced
1/2 cup shredded carrots
1 cup diced cooked potatoes
1 head of lettuce
1/3 cup salad oil or olive oil
1/4 cup cider vinegar
1 teaspoon salt
Pepper to taste
2 teaspoons sugar
1 teaspoon chili powder
1/4 teaspoon crumbled dried oregano
1 medium sized avocado
Juice of 1 lime
1/2 cup stuffed green olives

Sauté bread cubes in butter with the garlic until bread is golden brown; drain on paper toweling. Mix together lightly the celery, onion, green pepper, carrots, potatoes, and the croutons; heap in a salad bowl lined with lettuce leaves. Blend together the salad oil, vinegar, salt, pepper, sugar, chili powder, and oregano. Pour over salad and toss lightly. Garnish the top with slices of avocado sprinkled with lime juice and with stuffed olives cut in half. Serves 8.

Bean Sprout and Water Chestnut Salad

2 cups bean sprouts
1/4 cup water chestnuts, sliced

1/2 cup pineapple chunks
1/4 cup green pepper, slivered

Dressing:

1 cup mayonnaise
1 teaspoon soy

1 teaspoon curry powder

Use fresh bean sprouts if you can find them—they are much crisper than the canned. Clean sprouts well or drain the canned ones. Add water chestnuts, pineapple, and green pepper. Mix the dressing through the salad. Arrange salad in lettuce-lined bowl. Sprinkle toasted almonds over the top before serving. Serves 6.

Sliced Tomatoes With Roquefort Dressing

4 firm, ripe tomatoes
  Salad greens
1 Bermuda onion
1/4 cup minced parsley
1/4 cup crumbled Roquefort
  cheese

1/2 cup salad oil
2 tablespoons lemon juice
1 teaspoon salt
1/2 teaspoon sugar

Peel tomatoes and thinly slice crosswise; place on greens arranged on a large chop plate. Slice onion very thinly and place a slice on each tomato. Sprinkle with parsley. Blend together the Roquefort cheese, salad oil, lemon juice, salt, and sugar. Pour over tomatoes; chill at least 20 minutes before serving. Serves 6.

Cold 'n Crisp Salad

2 oranges, peeled, sliced, and
  slices cut in half
2 tomatoes, sliced and slices
  cut in half
1 green pepper, cut in slivers

3 green onions, sliced
5 radishes, sliced
1 cucumber, sliced
2 stalks of celery, sliced
  diagonally

Dressing:

1/3 cup vinegar
1/2 cup sugar
2/3 cup water

1/2 teaspoon salt
1/4 teaspoon pepper

Have oranges, vegetables, and dressing "refrigerator cold." Mix them together just before serving. Serve in side dishes—can be eaten with spoon if you want to enjoy dressing. Serves 4 to 6.

BREADS

Hot buttered French bread—with or without garlic—is a reliable stand-by for outdoor meals. For variety, however, you may wish to dress up your French bread in one of the ways described here. Rolls, rye, nut, and fruit breads are also delicious accompaniments to an outdoor meal.

Grilled French Bread

Cut sour French bread in half lengthwise and toast over the hot embers. Melt butter in shallow pan and dip the toasted bread into it.

Variation for garlic eaters:

Mince garlic and work into soft butter—spread on toasted French bread.

Hot Herb Bread

The bread is sourdough French, split the long way and toasted. For 2 big loaves, cream ½ pound butter, ¾ cup each minced chives and parsley, and ¼ cup minced sweet basil. Spread the bread while it is hot. Cut in 2-inch pieces. Serves 12.

French Bread Pizza Style

This French bread is a near relative to the popular pizza.

1 long loaf French bread	2 cans (2 oz. each) anchovy fillets
1 can (6 oz.) tomato paste	
¼ cup olive oil	½ pound Monterey jack or process American cheese, thinly sliced
½ teaspoon oregano	
Salt and pepper to taste	

Split loaf of French bread lengthwise in halves. Mix tomato paste, oil, oregano, salt, and pepper; spread on cut surface of bread. Lay anchovy fillets over tomato mixture, crosswise of the loaf; cover with slices of cheese. Place on baking sheet. Bake in a hot oven (450°) for 10 to 15 minutes to melt cheese. Cut crosswise.

Venetian Loaf

This treatment gives French bread a distinctly Italian flavor.

1 long loaf French bread
1/2 cup softened butter or margarine
1/2 cup grated Parmesan cheese
2 tablespoons olive oil
1/2 cup finely chopped parsley
1 clove garlic, finely chopped
1/2 teaspoon sweet basil
Salt to taste

Slash loaf of French bread crosswise in thick slices, cutting down to but not through the bottom crust. Blend butter and remaining ingredients together; spread between slices of bread. Wrap loaf in waxed paper or aluminum foil. Bake in a moderately hot oven (375°) for 15 to 20 minutes or until piping hot. Serve hot.

French Bread Monterey

Parmesan cheese, mayonnaise, and onion make a really robust loaf.

1 long loaf French bread
Softened butter or margarine
1 cup mayonnaise
1/2 cup grated Parmesan cheese
1/2 cup ground or finely chopped onion
1/2 teaspoon Worcestershire
Paprika

Cut loaf of French bread lengthwise in halves. Spread cut surfaces with butter. Place in oven to heat through. Meantime, mix all remaining ingredients except paprika; spread mixture on the hot bread; dust with paprika. Broil slowly until delicately browned. Cut crosswise.

Rye Bread With Eschalots

2 bunches eschalots, or
1 bunch green onions and
1 bunch chives
1 loaf rye bread (about 20 thin slices)
1 cube butter or margarine

Chop eschalots fine. Spread rye bread generously with butter that has been well creamed first. Then sprinkle each slice with the chopped eschalots and pile bread back in loaf form. Wrap first in wax paper, then in aluminum foil, and steam in oven at 275° for about 1½ hours—a little longer or shorter time will not matter. Serve very hot. Serves 8 to 10.

Crusty Rolls With Lemon-Parsley Butter

1 cube (½ cup) softened butter or margarine	2 tablespoons finely chopped parsley
1 tablespoon lemon juice	6 large French rolls

Blend together the butter, lemon juice, and parsley. Split rolls in half lengthwise and spread each half with the butter mixture. Place the halves together again and wrap each roll individually in aluminum foil. Place on the barbecue grill for 10 to 15 minutes, or until hot; turn once or twice. Or place in a moderately hot oven (375°) for 15 minutes.

Pastel De Elote

This can be served as a bread in lieu of the usual garlic bread at barbecues. You may make it in advance and reheat before serving.

½ pound butter or margarine	½ cup grated jack cheese
1 cup sugar	½ cup grated Tillamook cheese
4 eggs	¼ teaspoon salt
1 can (4 oz.) green chili peppers	1 cup flour
1 can (No. 303) cream style golden bantam corn	1 cup yellow cornmeal
	4 teaspoons baking powder

Cream butter and add sugar. Add eggs, one at a time, mixing in well. Chop peppers and add. Add corn and mix well. Add cheeses and pinch of salt. Sift flour and then measure; sift cornmeal and then measure; sift both together with baking powder and add to previous mixture. Pour into greased and floured glass baking dish (8 by 12 by 2 inches). Preheat oven at 350°. Reduce heat to 300° and bake for one hour. Serves 10.

Toasted Herb Roll in Loaf

1 loaf unsliced milk bread	¼ teaspoon savory
¾ cup butter	½ teaspoon thyme
¼ teaspoon salt	Cayenne
¼ teaspoon paprika	Other herbs as desired

Remove crusts from bread and slice through center lengthwise; then cut crosswise into about 2-inch squares—but not quite through. Spread with above mixture; tie loaf together and let stand. Heat in a slow oven (300°) 30 minutes or until it is warmed through. (Serve with *extra* paper napkins.)

Corn Barbecue Rolls

2 cups flour	2/3 to 1 cup milk
¾ teaspoon salt	1 can (12 oz.) whole kernel corn
4 teaspoons baking powder	Melted butter
4 tablespoons shortening	Paprika
1 egg, beaten	

Mix the dry ingredients and work in shortening. Add beaten egg and milk; mix to a soft dough. Place on a floured board, roll to ½-inch thickness, spread with drained corn, and brush over with melted butter.

Roll as for jelly roll and cut with a sharp knife into ½ to 1-inch slices. Place the slices, cut side down, on a cooky sheet, and dust with paprika. Bake in a 425° oven for about 15 minutes. Serve with country gravy, or simply as a bread with lots of butter. Makes 6 to 8 rolls.

RELISHES/ SIDE DISHES

Relishes are the taste-tantalizing side dishes that perk up any meal and add color and interest to the barbecue table. The central idea is variety—in color, texture, and flavor. And, of course, the relishes that you serve must complement the dishes that comprise the main part of the meal. They need not be elaborate, and they can all be prepared well ahead of the day of the barbecue.

Quick Meat Relish

1 large can (No. 2½) solid pack tomatoes	½ teaspoon each cloves and cinnamon
1 large onion chopped	1 teaspoon salt
¾ cup cider vinegar	Dash of cayenne or Tabasco
1 tablespoon sugar	

Empty tomatoes into a saucepan and cut through them so they will be in smaller pieces. Add the onion, vinegar, sugar, spices, salt, and cayenne to taste. Boil for about 15 minutes, or until slightly thickened. Makes about 3½ cups relish. Store relish in the refrigerator. Sliced celery or fresh or dehydrated green pepper may be added if desired.

Corn and Cabbage Relish

2½ cups fresh corn kernels (cut from approximately 5 ears)
3 cups shredded cabbage (approximately ¼ large head)
1 green pepper, diced
1 large onion, chopped
1 cup cider vinegar
½ cup sugar
¼ teaspoon turmeric
1½ teaspoons dry mustard
1 teaspoon salt
1 pimiento, diced

In a large kettle, combine corn, cabbage, green pepper, and onion. Add vinegar, sugar, turmeric, dry mustard, and salt, and mix thoroughly. Stirring occasionally, simmer for 45 minutes; then add pimiento. Pour into sterilized jars and seal immediately. Makes 3 pints. Excellent with barbecued chicken or ham.

Raw Tomato Relish

1 green chili pepper
1 large or 2 small tomatoes
1 small white onion
Salt

Place the green chili pepper on a fork and hold it over open flame until it is seared and the skin is broken. Then wrap in a dry towel for a few minutes to steam. Remove stem and skin, split, and remove *all* seeds (they contain most of the heat). Grind the pepper together with the tomatoes; add the onion. Serve at room temperature with beef, lamb, mutton, or fish. Serves 2 to 4.

Pepper Relish

6 large green peppers
2 canned green chili peppers
4 green onions (including tops)
1 small clove garlic, mashed or minced, or ¼ teaspoon garlic purée
1½ tablespoons lemon juice
2 teaspoons vinegar
2 teaspoons salad oil
1 teaspoon salt
½ teaspoon sugar
⅛ teaspoon pepper

Wipe green peppers with damp cloth, then bake them in a moderately slow oven (325°) for 45 minutes, or until peppers are just tender. Peel off any loose skin, then remove stems and seeds, and chop finely. Chop chili peppers and green onions and combine with chopped green peppers. Add garlic to pepper mixture along with lemon juice, vinegar, salad oil, salt, sugar, and pepper; then mix together thoroughly. Store in refrigerator. Makes 2 cups.

Green Tomato Barbecue Relish

2 cups ground green tomatoes (approximately 4 to 5)	2 small sweet red peppers, seeded and ground
2 cups ground peeled cucumbers (approximately 2 medium sized)	1 quart (4 cups) water
	1½ tablespoons salt
	2 cups sugar
2 cups ground onions (approximately 4 medium sized)	2 cups cider vinegar
	1 tablespoon mustard seed
3 medium sized tart apples, peeled and ground	6 tablespoons flour
	1 tablespoon dry mustard
1 green pepper, seeded and ground	¼ teaspoon turmeric

Mix together in a large kettle the prepared green tomatoes, cucumbers, onions, apples, green pepper, red peppers, water, and salt. Let stand for 24 hours; drain. Add sugar, 1½ cups of the vinegar, and mustard seed; bring to a boil. Make a paste of flour, dry mustard, and turmeric with the remaining ½ cup vinegar, and stir into boiling mixture. Stirring occasionally, simmer for 1½ hours. Pour into hot sterilized jars and seal immediately. Makes 4 pints.

Pickled Onion Relish

The mild-flavored, yellow-skinned sweet Spanish onion is your best choice for this relish. When the red Bermudas are in season, you might select them because of their bright color and mild flavor.

4 large onions, thinly sliced	¼ cup (4 tablespoons) mayonnaise
½ cup water	
1 cup vinegar	1½ teaspoons celery seed
1 tablespoon sugar	Salt

Place sliced onions in a shallow dish. Pour over the water and vinegar and sprinkle with the sugar; cover and chill for 4 hours. When you are ready to serve, drain the onions and mix together lightly with the mayonnaise, celery seed, and salt to taste. Serves 6.

Barbecue Potato Chips

To heat potato chips pile them in a wire popcorn popper and shake on garlic salt. Shake popper gently over the grill until the potato chips are hot and crisp. Then sprinkle with grated Parmesan cheese.

Barbecue Relish Plate

A barbecue relish plate is one easy way to handle the vegetable problem; it can also be a spectacular way. Select the most attractive large platter that you have, or any unusual shallow container that will hold the quantity needed. Choose the most beautiful raw vegetables that you can find in the market and chill them. Arrange them according to their contrasting colors and shapes so they are an eye-appealing selection.

Some of the most popular vegetables for such an arrangement include radish roses, stuffed celery stalks, carrot curls, thin cucumber and zucchini slices, tiny tomatoes, green onions, avocado wedges, and romaine hearts. Accompany the platter with a bowl of well-seasoned French or blue cheese dressing.

Another variation of the barbecue relish plate is a similar arrangement of marinated cooked vegetables, such as Brussels sprouts, lima or kidney beans, asparagus tips, artichoke hearts, baby beets and carrots, green or wax beans, broccoli and cauliflower sections, and tiny yellow crookneck squash.

Caraway-Garlic Pickled Beets

24 small young beets	1½ cups brown sugar, firmly packed
2 teaspoons salt	2 teaspoons whole caraway seeds
6 cups water	8 cloves garlic, cut in half
4 cups cider vinegar	

Scrub and trim beets, leaving on part of stem and all of root; then cook, covered, in boiling salted water for 45 minutes, or until tender. Cool beets in liquid; peel and cut into lengths the size of matchsticks. Return beet strips to pan with 4 cups of the cooking liquid; pour in vinegar, and add brown sugar, stirring until dissolved. Season with caraway seeds and garlic. Bring mixture to a full boil, simmer for 2 minutes, then dip out beets with slotted spoon and pack into sterilized jars, making certain to include 2 pieces of garlic and some caraway seeds in each jar. Boil liquid, then pour over beets; seal jars. Makes 4 pints.

The flavor improves as you let these tiny beets marinate in the caraway seed-garlic mixture. Toss the beets in a salad for a blaze of color, or serve with cuts of lamb or beef.

Pickled Prunes in Red Wine

A day or so before the dinner, fill a quart jar with prunes, pitted or not. Pour on, to cover, red wine that has been heated with pickling spices (use a teaspoon of spices to a cup of wine).

Apple Chutney

4 pounds apples	¾ cup raisins
2 quarts cider vinegar	1 large onion, chopped
1 to 2 cloves of garlic	2 pounds brown sugar
1 teaspoon salt	3 tablespoons salt
1 cup thinly sliced, pitted dates	1 teaspoon powdered ginger
¾ cup currants	1 teaspoon cayenne

Peel and core apples, then put through the food chopper, using the coarse blade. Place in a large kettle and pour over vinegar. Mash garlic with the 1 teaspoon salt, then stir into apple mixture. Add dates, currants, raisins, and onion, and let stand for 24 hours. Stir in brown sugar, salt, ginger, and cayenne. Stirring occasionally, simmer until thick—about 45 minutes. Pour into hot sterilized jars and seal. Makes 4 pints.

Mango Chutney

3¼ cups sliced, peeled mangoes (approximately 7 small mangoes)	2 tablespoons finely chopped garlic
2½ cups white sugar	4 tablespoons finely chopped green ginger or 2 tablespoons chopped dry ginger
1 cup brown sugar, firmly packed	1½ teaspoons salt
1 cup cider vinegar	1½ teaspoons whole cloves
½ cup seedless raisins	1½ small, dry, red chili peppers

Combine mangoes with white sugar and brown sugar; stir to mix well, then let stand overnight. In the morning remove the mangoes from the syrup that has formed. To the sugar syrup, add the vinegar, raisins, garlic, ginger, salt, and cloves. Snip the stems off the chili peppers and shake out seeds; crumble the peppers and add to the syrup mixture. Stirring occasionally, simmer for 30 minutes. Add the mangoes and continue cooking for 20 minutes. Pour into hot sterilized jars and seal. Makes 4 half pints.

Savory Butters

It is a good idea to make up several jars of flavorful butters and store them in the freezer, ready to serve with broiled steaks, hamburgers, and fish, and with roast corn, potatoes, and onions. Here are a few—some classics, some interesting variations:

Parsley-Lemon Butter, called *maitre d'hotel* in *haute cuisine,* is butter creamed with finely minced parsley and lemon juice. It does wonderful things for hamburgers, is almost a must with fish, and is good with steaks, chops, and liver.

Green Butter, or *beurre vert,* is butter creamed with pounded or extra well-minced parsley, chives, and sometimes other herbs. It is good with oysters roasted in the shell, and with broiled fish and charcoal-roasted lamb.

Anchovy Butter, which is butter mixed with anchovy paste, is extra good with broiled chops and steak, though it's good with fish, too. Try it with a roast of veal for a taste sensation.

Herb Butter lets you play your own tune. Cream butter with any herb or combination of herbs you choose, but remember not to overdo it. The fine herbs (*fines herbes*) are always safe: parsley, chives, tarragon, and sometimes chervil. To these may be added marjoram or thyme. This butter is used successfully for broiled chicken or turkey, and is good with roasted potatoes. Rosemary butter is nice with lamb chops, or with steak or fish. And oregano butter is delicious with corn or broiled tomatoes.

Bercy Butter, made with chopped shallots or green onions, is delightful on French bread and on corn. It's also good on steaks, chops, and broiled lobsters.

Chili Butter, made with chili powder, butter, and a drop of wine vinegar, seems to go particularly well with thick charcoal-broiled pork chops, or with roast corn or hamburgers.

Garlic Butter is so well known it is almost superfluous to mention it, but we do want to remind you that it has other uses than a spread for bread. Try it with London broil (broiled flank steak), grilled kidneys, or hamburgers. Try it on baked potatoes, too.